Game-Changing COACH

Game-Changing COACH

MINDFUL STRATEGIES FOR PEAK PERFORMANCE

Mary Fenerty Schumann, PhD

GAME-CHANGING COACH
MINDFUL STRATEGIES FOR PEAK PERFORMANCE

iUniverse books may be ordered through booksellers or by contacting:

iUniverse
1663 Liberty Drive
Bloomington, IN 47403
www.iuniverse.com
1-800-Authors (1-800-288-4677)

ISBN: 978-1-5320-3042-0 (sc)
ISBN: 978-1-5320-3041-3 (e)

Library of Congress Control Number: 2017912338

Print information available on the last page.

iUniverse rev. date: 01/08/2018

Contents

Acknowledgments vii

Introduction.. ix

Chapter 1:   Communication 1

Chapter 2:   Positive Coaching 19

Chapter 3:   Motivation..35

Chapter 4:   Goal Setting 47

Chapter 5:   Self-Efficacy and Confidence.................... 59

Chapter 6:   Team Cohesion... 71

Chapter 7:   Arousal and Anxiety 85

Chapter 8:   Choking 107

Chapter 9:   Slumps...117

Chapter 10: Mind-Set 127

Chapter 11: Parents and Technology..........................133

Chapter 12: Academic Performance 143

Closing.. 153

References 159

About the Author...173

Index... 175

Acknowledgments

I owe much to many people for encouraging me to write this book. First to the Ukrainian ice hockey coach who asked me where he could read about my work; you planted the seed. I have always loved to write but have struggled with believing that someone might want to read what I have to say. I decided to think of it as another form of teaching and training, two things I absolutely love to do. That approach, along with a lot of encouragement, helped me to do it.

To Michael, my boyfriend, and to Nancy, one of my best friends, thank you for your support and tolerance of my spending time away from fun in order to write. To my children, Kelly and Maggie, who listen to and encourage me, thank you. And to Mom and Dad, especially Mom, who told me she always loved to read what I write, thank you. In so many ways, I owe much about my love of learning to both of you, who provided a home and encouraged curiosity. I also have to thank my job coach, Charlene Rothkopf, who has been a never-ending source of support and encouragement. She held me to my commitments to work steadily toward my goal.

In addition, many thanks go to Debi Corbatto, the assistant athletic director at George Mason and a personal supporter of my goals. She fostered my work with the coaches at Mason and has always believed in me. And to my students and the athletes at Mason who have taught me much about their experiences through sharing themselves, thank you.

And to God, my ultimate support, who is ever present and helps me to become my best self. May my work glorify You.

Introduction

Coaching today's athletes is a challenging and demanding job but one ripe with opportunity. A coach's impact on young athletes' lives can be considerable. Coaching is a people job; good coaching requires a deep knowledge of both sport and human behavior. An ability to read or intuit what is going on with an athlete or a team, a finesse with spoken language, and an interest in developing people athletically and personally are all skills that great coaches possess. Additionally, coaches need to know how they come across to their athletes. Their verbal *and* nonverbal communication patterns color everything they do. Great coaches are highly skilled communicators.

In my work as a clinical and sport psychologist, helping teams develop as groups and improve their individual performance, I have observed many dynamics. At times, I have wanted to stop everything and talk to the coach about a concept or practice from the behavioral sciences. Often, there is not time or it is not appropriate to interrupt a practice or game. My goal in writing this book is to share a few things from the fields of psychology and sport psychology, as well as my experiences, that I believe increase the effectiveness of coaches. I have worked with a number of Division I teams, and I have taught sport psychology for almost ten years. In this book, I tried to be concise, and I tried not to make it academic. Most coaches, like their athletes, are doers and not as likely to be huge readers. My objective is to give coaches a little bit of research background but, more importantly, ideas on how to apply it.

Each chapter begins with a typical scenario from coaching life and then gives some information related to what we know about behavior. Each chapter then ends with coaching tips. Those sections contain the takeaways that are most relevant. When touring a college with my daughter a few years ago, I learned about Ben Franklin's view that knowledge is for service—and I want to turn some of what we know about topics like motivation, goal setting, and reinforcement into ideas about how to expand what you do. Good coaching translates into creating winning teams. Let's face it: we all prefer to win than lose, and many jobs depend on coaching success. You may be familiar with some of the concepts in this book, but what you read here might be the catalyst that charges your approach with new energy and ideas.

Part of my professional work involves giving presentations to coaches and athletes in a sports diplomacy program run by the US Department of State. The goal of this program is to increase dialogue and cultural understanding between people around the world, using sports as a platform to expose foreign athletes and coaches to American culture while providing them with an opportunity to establish links with US sports professionals and peers. After my presentations to participants in the sports diplomacy program, several coaches asked me if I had written something they could refer to. This book was partially born out of those requests.

As I mentioned, you may already be familiar with some of the information in this book, but a refresher course never hurts. In addition, I am confident that you will find new ideas that will help you assist the athletes you work with. The ideas and concepts in the following pages will give you the tools you need to ensure that athletes connect with themselves in ways that encourage mastery of their chosen sport, build their confidence, manage their emotions more effectively, and take more calculated risks on the field or court, which leads to winning games.

Young athletes today—while not integrally different from youth of the past—live in a more connected, multitasking environment than most of us from previous generations. They were born into a time of cell phones, internet, and social media, with tremendous digital connectedness. This inherent difference in their world affects their familial and other social relationships, their sense of self and development of independence, and their academic lives. I believe technology also impacts their athletic relationships as well. One coach told me that his athletes never talked to each other on the bus driving to games, preferring to have headphones on. Walk into any college classroom, and all eyes are pointed downward toward screens. Much communication between athletes and their peers and coaches is done electronically. As a psychologist, I have wondered if young people of this generation are as skilled at reading facial cues and subtle communication as those of their parents' generation. They often prefer to text than to call, so cryptic verbal communication is their norm.

I hope to highlight some of these issues that affect how our young people relate to each other and to their coaches, which may arise from their lifestyles as millennials.

I also touch on mindfulness meditation in a few different chapters in this book. "Mindfulness is about being fully aware of whatever is happening in the present moment, without filters or the lens of judgment" (Stahl and Goldstein 2010). It has also been defined as a mental state achieved by focusing one's awareness on the present moment while acknowledging and accepting one's feelings, thoughts, and bodily sensations. Although mindfulness-based stress reduction (MBSR) was developed by Jon Kabat-Zinn as a technique to help those suffering from chronic stress due to medical conditions, more recently it has been applied to people who wish to improve focus and attention in order to perform optimally. A few coaches, particularly Phil Jackson, former coach of the Lakers and former president of the Knicks, have used this method with their teams. Jackson's mindfulness trainer, George Mumford, recently wrote a book called *The Mindful Athlete* (Mumford 2015), describing its use with regard to helping athletes perform more optimally.

I discovered mindfulness meditation at a time when I was going through tremendous stress in my life. I was attending a basic meditation class at the university where I teach, and a wise person suggested that I try to start a daily practice. What I discovered in meditation was a peacefulness that transformed my ability to cope with many stressful life changes. My personal practice affected my desire to teach my clients, students, athletes, and teams. I have been using mindfulness exercises in my sport psychology classes for five years, asking students to reflect on these exercises weekly in an online journal.

In addition, I have taught several Division I athletic teams to use these exercises as a way to focus on the present moment, connect with their bodies, and reduce the noise and chatter in their heads. While there are many suggestions in this book, I hope that coaches will take a hard look at this practice for the purpose of teaching athletes this tool to help them focus their attention, quiet their minds, and regulate emotion. You may also find that it helps you to be a more grounded and clear-thinking coach. For an interesting approach to training coaches in mindfulness meditation, see Kat Longshore's dissertation research (Longshore 2015). Her work is innovative and seminal in her attempts to bring this approach to coaches in order to help them manage stressful emotions and be present in their work.

While my book will cover a number of topics, I want you to take a fresh look at your own coaching, grab some new ideas and practices, and strengthen your approach to help your athletes and teams perform at a higher level. Communicating more effectively, helping athletes to focus their attention on the here and now, and creating uplifting environments that motivate your team will help you to enjoy your work and win more games. Have fun with this!

Chapter 1

COMMUNICATION

You are trying to conduct practice, and the players are just not with you. You talk to them, try to get through to them, but it's like their heads are somewhere else. *Why can't I convince them to take this time seriously? How are we supposed to improve if they are not even paying attention or giving me their best?* You ask them to do a straightforward drill. One of the guys, Alec, is never in the right place. You have directed him over and over again. *What's with this guy?*

"Alec, you're never in the right place at the right time! Did you even hear what I said? How many times do I have to say the same thing? Do you guys ever pay attention?"

***

On a different day, it's the same scenario. But today you're feeling good, and the guys' behavior, while annoying, is not getting to you. You have just witnessed the above scenario. This time, however, you say, "Guys, please listen. You've tried this repeatedly, but somehow you're not getting the gist of this. I believe you want to do this correctly. Alec, you're the leader on this drill. Tell the guys who keep missing their positions where to go. Let's try again."

Two responses to the same situation: one team feels aggravated and thinks the coach is a jerk; the other team hears encouragement and belief. The first message produces frustration, whereas the second message inspires effort. We are not always going to do everything right as coaches, but repeatedly responding in a way that puts the players down will produce poor results for your team. This chapter will consider the impact of styles of communication on teams. It is taken from research on parenting. Authoritarian, authoritative, and permissive parenting styles will be discussed as they relate to coaching. These different styles determine a parent's approach to discipline, tone of communication, and extent of limit setting. Coaches have a similar job, and these styles have implications for approaches to coaching. In addition, positive communication will be discussed as it relates to coaching. Research on positive communication has demonstrated its enormous ability to motivate people and create a helpful team climate.

Through my observations of teams, I believe communication to be the most important factor in the team's cohesion, ability to work together, and overall well-being. Competitive teams that win always seem to communicate well on the court or field. There are many verbal and nonverbal gestures that send messages of support and encouragement. Some players have a particularly critical role with regard to communication (e.g., point guards in basketball, quarterbacks in football, sweepers in soccer). When you watch a team that plays well, you see players who lead and rally the group, communicate often, and encourage effort.

> The coach has a vital role in establishing communication norms on a team. How open, supportive, and positive a coach is with his or her players has a huge impact on the team. Coach Pat Summitt, the former coach of the University of Tennessee women's basketball team, said:
>
> "Open, honest communication is the most important element in building trust within the program. The head coach must take the leadership role in establishing an open communication policy." (Summitt and Jenkins 1998)

Coach-to-player communication is established early in the relationship between the player and the coach during recruitment or tryouts. Another critical time in the communication process between coach and players is when you gather the team for the first meeting each season; you set a tone, communicate an attitude, and establish ground rules. Additionally, you communicate goals, expectations, and feelings. What you say and *how* you say it in this first meeting is critical.

Excellent coaches are great communicators. Having an open-door policy or creating an atmosphere where athletes can always talk to you as a coach is essential and will deliver big rewards in the long run. There is a parallel process that happens between coach and players and then player to player. For example, in families, when spouses communicate well and get along, the impact is felt in the family. These kids have a great model and feel comfortable communicating with their parents. Among teams, coaches who value their assistant coaches and players are always interested in their input, feedback, and ideas. I have witnessed situations where coaches say that they want feedback from the players, but they do not really listen, take it in, or respond to it. Let's face it: being available and interested in players' input takes energy, time, openness, and a willingness to respond. In addition, it takes a nondefensive attitude to consider your own behavior. Not all coaches want that type of relationship with their players, because it gives the players power and influence. But it also generates huge amounts of trust and respect from the players toward the coach.

Authoritarian, Authoritative, and Permissive Styles of Coaching: Implications from Parenting Research

I believe teams are much like families due to the power structure of coaches and players and the fact that most of us have the family as our model for learning about communication. Some of the research on styles of parenting has implications for coaching. Through her research, Diana Baumrind studied the impact of different styles of parenting on adolescents and their behavior. She distinguished between three parenting styles: authoritarian, authoritative, and permissive parenting (Baumrind 1966; Baumrind 1991; Darling 1999). The two main factors she looked at were parental responsiveness and parental expectations.

Authoritarian Parenting

Authoritarian parenting has the attitude of "my way or the highway," is low in responsiveness toward kids, and is high on demands. Because kids are taught to follow rules rather than take initiative, they are more capable of following instructions than becoming leaders. They are taught what to think rather than how to think. The parent with the authoritarian style more often uses punishment, and certainly we have witnessed examples of coaches that adopt this style. Many of us have watched the Bobby Knights of this world, or men like Coach Carter or Coach Boone from *Remember the Titans*. All of these demonstrated an authoritarian style of coaching, also known as the dictator style. When there is a lot of conflict between players, or the players come from chaotic backgrounds, this style can be helpful in establishing order and structure. However, Baumrind's research looked at the impact of authoritarian parenting on kids as they grew up and found that they were more passive and emotionally dependent, more fearful, and less socially skilled. They also felt more anger, which sometimes emerged as more rebellion against parents or parental figures. This suggests that coaches who are highly controlling in their style and communication may inadvertently create feelings of rebellion in their players. Moreover, an authoritarian style of coaching may also cause players to take less initiative, be more passive but also rebellious, and be less able to deal with adults. Coaches of adolescents and young adults have to consider how this style affects what they are trying to cultivate in their athletes.

Recent research on coaches' use of psychological control has yielded interesting results. Athletes who saw their coaches as high in psychological control (which means coaches who used pressure or authoritarian behaviors to impose a specific way of acting on an individual) showed higher levels of the following: depressive symptoms, disordered eating, and burnout (Bartholomew et al. 2011). There were also negative effects on emotion among athletes with coaches who were seen as having high psychological control, as well as the thwarting of innate psychological needs (Bartholomew et al. 2011). Again, these are not desirable outcomes in athletes; coaches would do best to choose their communication styles carefully, with an eye toward what patterns of communication produce the best results between coaches and athletes.

Authoritative Parenting

Authoritative style parenting (also called democratic) is high on responsiveness but also high on expectations. Research shows that adolescents do well psychologically with this type of parenting, showing responsible and self-assured behavior (Baumrind 1966). This data is relevant to coaching since parenting and coaching are similar processes; teams are like families. Authoritative parents are warm toward kids but firm on expectations. Rules are clear, but there may be dialogue with kids or adolescents, tolerating occasional challenges to authority, or explanations of rules. Although authoritative and authoritarian parents are equally high in behavioral control, authoritative parents tend to be low in psychological control, while authoritarian parents tend to be high (Darling 1999). Ultimately, we want young adults to respect authority but also learn to negotiate with their bosses or authority figures. In this way, they take initiative and have the experience of being heard, of trying to get what they want, even if they don't always achieve their goals. They do not feel as oppressed by this type of parent or authority figure. In terms of teams, coaches with this style may get more cooperative behavior from their athletes and less rebellion. This could mean asking athletes or your team how they feel about something, soliciting their input about rules when setting up teams, and engaging them in the process of communication about the workings of the team. A certain amount of engagement with the athletes in terms of granting them a feeling of control could pay big dividends. This increases a sense of ownership because players feel that they have an element of control. With this style, I think of John Wooden and Coach K—tough but warm, with limits and high expectations for their teams.

Permissive Parenting

The permissive style of parenting is exactly as it sounds— the parent is high on responsiveness but low on expectations.

It has also been called the laissez-faire style of parenting. Parents with this style indulge their children. The response of this style of parenting on young people is greater conformity to their peers, but they are not as responsible for their own actions, and they can be disorganized. Young adults need structure and limits, guidelines that let them know what a coach's expectations are. Being too easy on players does not result in respect for authority, since the limits are not clear. Being too friendly with players or needing their approval may result in problems with players developing a lack of respect for the coach. Starting the season with a warm but firm style and clear limits establishes authority early on. Later, there is time to relax and increase responsiveness to players. If one starts too easy, one will not gain the needed respect.

More recent considerations of parenting styles have been discussed by Stephen Greenspan, who suggests an expansion of Diana Baumrind's two-factor model of demandingness and responsiveness. He introduced the concept of tolerance, which he finds allows for important situational flexibility. In his view, the child needs limits, but sometimes it's more important to keep family harmony. Applied to coaching, this suggests that coaches need to make momentary decisions about whether to hold fast to rules or to allow team harmony to be the dominant value. In another perspective on Baumrind's theory, Catherine Lewis (1981) claimed that what is so vital to authoritative parenting is not the high control; it's the respect for the children. Applied to coaching, this would imply that a respect for players, some degree of control but the ability to be flexible, and a concern for the harmony of the team are critical. With regard to coaching, I believe that the authoritative style would be a beneficial approach with older adolescent or young adult athletes. These are coaches who are warm and responsive to their athletes but who also have high demands. I think it is important for coaches to be in control but not overly controlling. Coaches who choose this style of authority may be the most helpful in teaching young adult athletes to express concerns, openly communicate with the coach, and commit to hard work. This in no way means that the coach is a doormat. Contrary to that, the coach is firm on issues he or she feels strongly about (e.g., standards related to practice rules and games) but potentially interested in suggestions the players might have about how the team could improve or practice more efficiently.

Communication in Coaching

A common complaint among players regarding communication with coaches is that they do not know what the coach is thinking, or they would like to have more feedback. Incomplete information is often at the root of problematic relationships. This is also true between coaches and players. Athletes who are not playing should know *why* they are not playing; they should also understand their role on the team. Setting up regular meetings with players individually is often helpful. It does not have to take a long time. Five to ten minutes of solo meeting time every few weeks with a coach can be just what an athlete needs. In these meetings, a coach can tell players what they are doing well, what needs more work, and something about their role on the team. Helping less-skilled or less-experienced players to feel valued and important to the team keeps them hopeful and working hard.

An example of this occurred between my daughter and one of her high school coaches. In my daughter's sophomore year, she had hoped to make the varsity soccer team. Instead, she was listed on the junior varsity team. Needless to say, she was disappointed. The coach, however, totally turned the situation around. She told my daughter she was a leader, that she needed her work ethic on the JV team and that she was certain that she would be on varsity in the following season. My daughter walked away from that communication feeling valued as opposed to not good enough.

Something I have observed in watching different coaches communicate is that some coaches seem to enjoy withholding information. This is truly a power issue and often creates anxiety among players. Where it is appropriate, sharing information helps players know what is going on. For example, making a lot of last-minute changes to practice times disrespects the athletes' and assistant coaches' schedules. Some coaches seem to enjoy this type of power. However, it does not make for good relationships or a sense of the athlete's well-being. Consistency and reliability are important factors in developing trust between young athletes and coaches. Coaches who do what they say and say what they do are likely to create strong relationships and a sense of trust on their teams. The foundation of good relationships is trust, and this is no different on a team. Clear, consistent communication helps to build trust.

Another interesting dilemma in coaching is when coaches think they communicated a concept to their players, but when the players are asked about it, they do not recall the idea ever being discussed. This is a big problem. One solution when you teach something to your players or tell them about an important policy is to ask players to repeat back to you what they heard you say. This advice is often given to sales executives and corporate leaders to help them communicate clearly. This is a key process with good communicators, because you want to be sure that the receivers are actually hearing the message. If you are unsure about whether your team or a player heard you correctly, ask.

Another suggestion is to be direct. Do not beat around the bush. Talk directly to the person you wish to hear the communication, rather than sending messages through another player or coach. Also, be thorough in your communication. Make sure you give details if they are necessary. For example, "When you did X during the game, it caused an error that resulted in a foul. It cost us X points and turned the ball over to our opponent. You need to avoid this in the future."

Verbal Communication

Verbal communication refers to the spoken language as well as sounds used to convey a message. This is in contrast to using gestures or mannerisms to communicate something. Verbal communication can take two forms, written and oral. Thus a coach could give pregame, halftime, or postgame speeches to the whole team, meet with individual athletes, yell orders, correct mistakes, and discuss strategy at practice. He or she could email, send texts, or make phone calls. Reports of stats are also another form of verbal communication. The spoken word influences the context and content of all of these. In spite of what you say, how you say it (tone, inflection, loudness, and emotionality) affects the interpretation of the message. As an example, some coaches always raise their voices and are perceived to be angry by the volume of their voice, when they do not think they are. Loudness and the speed at which you say something can communicate some level of aggressiveness or anxiety. When people are calm, they tend to speak slowly. Speaking quickly conveys urgency and, at times, anxiety. In the heat of the moment, keeping a businesslike tone of voice might be more effective because it can communicate a level of seriousness and trust. It is not overly emotional. Try to take a mindful, deep breath before responding if you would like to have greater control when communicating.

Nonverbal Communication

Nonverbal communication is communication without words or language, as is used in oral or written communication. It utilizes gestures, facial expressions, eye contact, physical proximity, and touching for communicating with others. Nonverbal communication is learned in childhood: it may be taught or passed on to you by your parents or caregivers, as well as others with whom you have contact. We say that it is culturally determined, and different gestures can mean different things across cultures. Nonverbal communication is thought to be unconscious or below one's level of awareness, which also means that it can come across quickly. When you grow up in a particular society, you adopt the subtleties and mannerisms of your cultural group.

Some communication experts believe that most communication is nonverbal. How we sit or stand, how we hold our arms, whether our posture is upright or slumped— all of these transmit information. Examples of positive nonverbal communication are a smile, pat on the back, nod of the head, or thumbs-up. Gestures such as pointing or shaking a fist can be perceived as aggressive or angry. Fidgeting or constant movement can convey nervousness or anxiety. Both verbal and nonverbal communication can also be forms of reinforcement, which will be discussed in the next chapter. Your facial expressions often reveal how you really feel, sending vital information to your team. Make good eye contact with athletes or team members when you speak to them. Stand up straight and tall to convey authority and power. Move slowly and deliberately rather than frenetically if you wish to communicate confidence as opposed to anxiety or fear. All of these subtle and not so subtle movements express messages to the recipient. If what you say and how you say it are at odds, players will tend to believe your nonverbal behavior as more authentic to your actual feelings.

You can also teach your players about what their own nonverbal behavior communicates on the court or field. Amy Cuddy's research on body language reveals that we can change other people's perceptions and our own body chemistry by changing our body positions (see https://www.ted.com/speakers/amy_cuddy). Teach athletes to hold themselves tall and keep their heads up even after making a mistake. Their nonverbal behavior communicates information to the team they are competing with.

Your team members should understand that the nature of communication during games is different from during practices. There is less time to communicate a message during time-outs and between periods or quarters. I watched a women's basketball coach call her team out on a time-out and deliver a loud, commanding instruction that definitely caught their attention (along with the spectators'!). It had to do with effort, and it was highly insistent. But it was respectful. I then watched the team go out and play much harder. Her firm stance, corrective feedback, and energy motivated them. Although coaches have varying styles, and some may not raise their voices during time-outs, I would hope that their tone of urgency, their energy, and their command are clearly noticed by their players.

A coach's credibility will affect how well the players hear what he or she has to say. In his book, *Successful Coaching* (2014), Rainer Martens suggests that the following things hurt credibility:

- The coach doesn't seem knowledgeable about what he or she says.
- What the coach says makes little sense or is of no importance to the players.
- The coach often distorts things or simply lies and inspires little trust in them.
- The coach constantly speaks negatively.
- The coach speaks to athletes as though they were stupid or less important than they are.

If there is one mistake that coaches often make with higher-level players, it is speaking down to them. Young people who are playing at a higher level (college, for example) have been playing their sport for many years. They have had numerous coaches, and they have a set of experiences that informs what they think and do. If you speak to them as though they are idiots, they will feel it, and they will not respect or trust you. That said, players are not your peers, and they need you to have authority over them. Finding the sweet spot between respecting them as young adults but maintaining your position as their leader is critical.

Finding Your Sweet Spot

Finding your own voice in terms of how you communicate with athletes and your team takes time. Most important is to be yourself. Each of us has a unique personality, and this can contribute much to our typical communication style. How were you coached? What did you like about your coaches' styles? What didn't you like? Some of us were coached by our parents. I have often asked students to reflect on their best coaches, and many times they will tell me that the toughest coaches communicated support but also demanded a lot of their players and teams. An attitude of respect is essential, and I personally believe that some psychological distance is necessary when working with teams. You cannot be their best friend, but you can be an important, caring adult in their lives who knows a lot about them. They can also learn from you and will be interested in your life and stories that you share from your experiences. But you need to be in charge, and this requires some distance in order to be an authority figure. Adopting an attitude of experimentation can also be helpful. What happens when you are firm with your team, or tough? How does the team respond when you express more support? Do you ever joke with the team? I think of a fishing reel in this situation, sometimes sending out more line, and other times reeling it in. Trust yourself. Ask your assistant coaches for feedback.

Staying Positive

Another common mistake is too much negativity. This creates poor morale among the team. You wouldn't choose to hang out with friends who were always saying negative things to each other. One cannot overemphasize the importance of positive, constructive communication in building the kind of team young athletes want to be a part of. If the coach has nothing good to say about the individual athletes or the team's performance, then the players will get discouraged. Always try to find something to praise. Barbara Frederickson, a psychologist who studied with Martin Seligman, the father of positive psychology in this country, has done research on the impact of positive communication on couples, families, and organizations. She says that a 3:1 ratio of positive to negative communication is needed and recommends a 5:1 ratio for optimal functioning (Frederickson 2009). So if you have corrected your team three times already this practice, you need to find nine things they have done well to balance it out and keep the emotional climate positive.

Kim Cameron, from the University of Michigan business school, has studied individuals who have high impact on their organizations. He has found that influential individuals in the workplace have many connections to others and that their communication is highly positive. He also found that there is a strong relationship between energy and communication, stating that everything alive has a tendency to move toward positive energy and away from negative energy (Cameron 2012).

Positive, encouraging communication is not just for young players; college-level athletes need it too. When it is done well, athletes can incorporate these positive messages into their own thoughts and become their own supporter in the quiet moments before competition or during critical plays. Say what you mean and mean what you say. And keep most of your communication positive!

Coaching Communication Tips

- Have a team meeting during which players help build the rules for conduct and standards of the team.

- Keep an open-door policy with your players and assistant coaches; you want their input.

- Identify what they are doing right and praise, praise, praise!

- Try to meet with players individually for five to ten minutes to tell them what they do well, what needs more work, and what their role is on the team (every couple weeks, if possible).

- When giving negative feedback, find something positive and deliver that first. Then follow it with critical feedback. Finish it with another positive comment. This is known as the sandwich method.

- Keep communication during games short and to the point.
- Try to keep positive to negative communications to a 3:1 ratio.
- Be honest and authentic in your communication.
- Respect your players in the way you speak to them and treat them.
- Watch your tone of voice. *How* you say something is as important as *what* you say.
- Try to build an authoritative style, not an authoritarian style (dictator style) of coaching. This means rules are clear and firm but that athletes can discuss or approach you if they have ideas or legitimate issues with a rule.
- Avoid a permissive style of coaching. An absence of limits and rules creates chaos, and too much freedom can also create rebellion or problem behavior.

Chapter 2

POSITIVE COACHING

"Wow—that's close! You guys are slowly getting this drill! Steven, get closer to the post. Jose, you're exactly where I want you to be. Ronnie, stay on the forward. Good effort! Let's do it again!"

Versus:

"What did I just say! You guys can't pay attention to save your lives. How many times have I told you to place yourselves in better position to perform that drill? Steven, you're never close enough to the post. Devon, you never move fast enough! What are you guys doing out there? Daydreaming?"

After reading these comments, how do you feel? One set of remarks motivates effort; the other shoots it down.

Obviously, we cannot always respond as the coach did in the first example as opposed to the second. But when we can, there is much power to reinforcing what is right and inspiring effort. This chapter will first explore the best ways of giving constructive feedback to your players, including the use of reinforcement or rewards for different levels of athletes. Understanding and using reinforcement effectively can contribute to better management of your team. Certain forms of reinforcement also affect motivation, which will be discussed in the next chapter. Additionally, this chapter will explore how to develop rules for your team and the process of involving athletes. Lastly, the final part of the chapter will review methods of giving feedback, as well as ideas for how to do that properly. These principles of behavior are something many people take for granted. But they are powerful tools for motivating and affecting human behavior. Because good coaching involves constant teaching and instruction, a refresher on some of these learning concepts will be helpful for you to get the best from your athletes and teams. Getting the best means winning more games!

Positive Reinforcement

The essence of positive reinforcement originates from Thorndike's law of effect (Thorndike 1905), which says that actions that are followed by satisfying (rewarding) consequences tend to be repeated in the situation in which they occur. Actions followed by dissatisfying (or punishing) consequences tend to not be repeated in the situation. Later, B. F. Skinner studied the frequency of reinforcing behavior. He studied schedules of reinforcement, or different patterns of applying positive reinforcement to create learned behaviors. He differentiated between four different patterns, or schedules, of reinforcement: fixed ratio, variable ratio, fixed interval and variable interval. What he found was that animals produced different patterns of behavioral responses depending on how often they received reinforcers (in this case, food pellets). When the reinforcer is removed, the learned response will disappear or become extinct (the term Skinner used for what happens when a learned behavior stops).

In *continuous reinforcement*, the desired behavior is reinforced every time it occurs. This schedule is best used early on in the stages of learning, in order to create a strong association between the behavior and the response. Thus, a coach who is teaching a new skill or drill would praise the players every time they executed the skill correctly.

Partial reinforcement involves responding to a behavior with reinforcement only part of the time. Although it takes longer to learn a behavior with this pattern of reinforcement, the behavior is more resistant to extinction (this means it is not forgotten quickly). Skinner found that behaviors reinforced on partial schedules persist a lot longer than those reinforced on a continuous schedule (Skinner 1969). The following is a brief summary of the different ways of reinforcing a behavior using a partial schedule.

- *Fixed-ratio schedule:* This schedule produces a high, steady rate of responding with only a short pause after the delivery of the reinforcer. An example of a fixed-ratio schedule would be delivering a treat to your dog after he sits in response to your command four times. So every four times he sits when commanded, he gets a treat.

- *Variable-ratio schedule:* A response is reinforced after an unpredictable number of responses. An example would be the type of response a person gets when he or she plays the slot machines. Sometimes it takes three pulls to win; other times it takes fifteen. The result is a high and steady rate of responding.

- *Fixed-interval schedule:* The first response is rewarded only after a specified amount of time has elapsed. This schedule causes high amounts of responding near the end of the time period. An example of this in a sports setting would be praising an athlete with verbal praise and a pat on the back the first time he or she does a skill (such as a three-point shot in basketball) within a fifteen-minute time block. The coach would not praise again until another fifteen minutes has gone by and the player again does the skill correctly. A coach would again praise the player the first time he or she makes the shot in the second fifteen-minute time block.

- *Variable-interval schedule:* This occurs when a response is rewarded after an unpredictable amount of time has passed. The result of this schedule is a slow, steady rate of responding. An example of this would be praising a player verbally after the first successful foul shot following a one-minute interval, another praise after the first successful foul shot after a five-minute time period, and again praising the player after a two-minute time block.

Enough psychology—what does this have to do with coaching? Basically, coaches need to think about *what* they do to reinforce athletes and *how often* they reinforce them. B. F. Skinner, one of the greatest thinkers and inventors of behavioral theory, felt he could create any talent if he could understand the reinforcers that the person most cared about. How well you respond to behavior on your team will affect the mood of the players, the motivational climate of your team, how well they comply with your rules, and ultimately, and most importantly, how well they perform as a group. While the connection may seem obtuse at times as we go into detail about these concepts, how well you manage and influence a group of young people will directly impact whether they will develop as a winning team.

Rewards or reinforcers come in many forms. There are verbal and nonverbal reinforcers like praise or exuberant expressions ("Yes!"). Nonverbal reinforcers are a smile, pat on the back, nod of the head, or thumbs-up. There are many nonverbal ways of expressing both approval and disapproval (the shake of the head, the frown, and the silent-but-deadly look community disapproval). Not so subtle are the cursing, muttering under the breath, or pounding something nearby. Speaking positively to the whole team about an individual or the team's performance is another means of verbal reinforcement. Other forms of rewards are a day off from practice or a choice of activity. Food is a wonderful reinforcer; most athletes are always hungry, so a special dinner or reward of that nature often works.

One of the most important aspects of reinforcement is that it should follow soon after the demonstration of a desirable behavior or skill. So if your team has done something well, or an athlete has completed a tough skill he or she has not done before, you want to react quickly. Positive reinforcement works best if it is right after the behavior.

In addition, negative reinforcement is doing something to remove something unpleasant or to stop a certain behavior. For example, turning off your alarm clock in the morning is negative reinforcement. By pressing the *stop* button, the noise of the alarm goes away. If a player has performed poorly or made a penalty, and the coach pulls him or her out of the game, losing playing time is an unpleasant experience. Making players sprint or run suicides when they are late are examples of punishment.

Punishment

Many coaches wonder about the utility of punishment in sport. Certainly we have all had the experience of being forced to run sprints when the team wasn't putting out effort in practice. But what is the scoop on punishment? Is there a place for it in coaching? My own viewpoint is that punishment should be used selectively and not that often. I am not talking about quick verbal correction that is negative, such as "No! That's not it. Try again." I reserve the word *punishment* to mean something aversive that does not feel good that is in response to behavior that the coach does not wish to see repeated. That said, several athletes have reported that occasional punishment was effective because it let the team know that what they were doing was unacceptable. I think if a coach has earned the respect of the players and has a good foundation in terms of the relationships, punishment can be used carefully and hopefully selectively to clearly let the team or a player know that they have stepped outside of what is acceptable in terms of their actions (or lack thereof).

That said, we know that positive reinforcement is a powerful motivator, and some youth coaches are encouraged to use an 80:20 ratio of positive reinforcement to punishment ratio (Williams and Krane 2015). Generally, positive reinforcement is considered a more effective technique because it motivates players to perform the desired behaviors. Whereas, one of the undesirable side effects of punishment is that it can cause a fear of failure and can reduce how much an athlete enjoys the activity. Competition can be seen as threatening instead of a challenge (Smith, Smoll, and Passer 2002). Athletes with higher fear of failure are more prone to choke under pressure, because they focus on the feared consequences rather than on what needs to be done. Interestingly, players who started with low self-esteem benefited the most from positive coaching techniques (Smith, Smoll, and Curtis 1979).

With young players, coaches seem to understand that athletes need encouragement to learn difficult skills. Praising players each time they do something correctly is helpful early on in skill development. As they learn the skill, praising them occasionally is more effective. They receive their own feedback from the results of the skilled movement (e.g., the ball goes in the basket, or they hit the ball at bat). Older and more competitive athletes still need some instruction but need to be coached in positive terms and language. They may not need as much positive reinforcement as young athletes, but they need encouragement and continued prompting to work hard. People work for rewards, and we all want to be recognized for our efforts. Positive reinforcement is contagious, creates energy, and fuels effort. Coaches who reward *effort* and not just outcome *get increased work* from their teams.

Additionally, positive reinforcement has been studied in regard to teaching certain skills or plays. In a study by Komaki and Barnett (1977) on the use of positive reinforcement when teaching football plays, they divided players into three groups. Each group was taught a different play. In the reinforcement group, each time the team executed a part of the play correctly, they were told so and reinforced. In the other two groups (control groups), no reinforcement was given for the correct execution of the play. The study showed that the group in which players were reinforced executed the play correctly significantly more often than the groups that did not get reinforced. This shows that using positive reinforcement to teach skilled movement in sport improves learning.

Continuous effort that goes unrewarded can create a sense of helplessness, which over time can contribute to feelings of depression or discouragement. Athletes have shared their discouragement with me when they do not know what they need to do to improve their play or to be able to get playing time. This lack of communication and understanding between the player and coach about what they do and the desired gains (e.g., playing time, improvement) creates a sense of passiveness and hopelessness among players. If a player is not skilled enough to achieve playing time, he or she should understand their role and what he or she needs to improve and work toward in order to gain playing time as a nonstarter or one who is being groomed for future seasons. The last thing a coach wishes to create in his or her players is a passive attitude toward improvement.

Rewarding small accomplishments such as incremental increases in speed, strength, percentages, or stats is a wonderful means of noticing progress on the way to further achievements. Having athletes track their progress toward short-term goals using notebooks and making positive comments on these achievements is a good way to notice what's right. Coaches can reward character and qualities like good sportsmanship to create the kind of team behavior that they would like to establish.

Work ethic is an important quality to watch for and reward. Having a weekly achievement of highest effort among players can create some healthy competition to put out maximal effort. One exercise I have seen a coach do at a team meeting is to have players "reward" their teammates for things like "great attitude," "mental toughness," or "great work ethic." Sometimes they create small certificates or simple cards, something tangible. Athletes often feel pride receiving these acknowledgments from their peers. One coach said that when she was a college athlete, she was recognized for her work ethic; this designation kept her working hard even when she was tired, because she wanted to uphold her standing with her teammates. This method of positive reinforcement generates an upbeat team climate and increases motivation.

Setting Rules

Creating structure and rules on a team sets expectations from the start, and hopefully players are involved in that to some degree. When players feel they have an influence in creating rules, they may feel more ownership and may exhibit a greater degree of compliance with the rules. There is some research that a more democratic approach to teams creates a better morale on the team (Smith and Smoll 2008). Obviously, age, maturity, and a team's history and members must be considered. Rules are most effective when they describe what an athlete is supposed to do (e.g., be at practice on time, dressed and ready, be respectful to coaches and teammates). There are practice rules and game rules. If at all possible, a coach can involve players in coming up with some of the rules. Compliance may be higher when the players take ownership of the rules and agree to abide by them.

At a minimum, players should be able to hear what a coach's rules are and understand his or her expectations. They should also be aware of the consequences of breaking the rules. If you as a coach are not going to stand by your team rules or enforce them, don't bother wasting your time. There is nothing more ineffective than a leader who doesn't follow through, and it does not generate respect between you and your team. You can have a policy of one warning, but if the athlete breaks the rule after that warning, consequences should be clear and immediate. Otherwise, rules are not going to impact behavior. (Remember that the most effective rewards and punishments follow behavior almost immediately.)

Another key point is that you need to enforce the rules consistently with all players. Starting players should not be excused from consequences of their actions on a team. This can create anger and resentment toward the coach and the teammate who is spared because of his or her ability level. Teams are like families, and all parents know that young people like to be treated justly and will notice right away if a sibling gets more privileges or gets away with things.

Your rules should comply with any larger governing organization that has power over your team. Thus, if you are a college-level coach, your rules should be in agreement with the athletic department at your college or university, as well as the NCAA. If you are a high school coach, your rules should be in sync with the school and the league, county, district or state in which you compete. A youth coach has to comply with the town, county league, or travel league in which they play. You can also have your rules printed up and have athletes sign a code of conduct. This is one way of communicating the rules and making sure you have something to refer to when there are problems.

Feedback

"Pass the ball! Can't you see that your teammate is waiting at the post? Are you even looking?"

Or,

"When you miss the shot, don't waste another breath. I can see you get down on

yourself. You look down and shake your
head. What are you thinking? Where is
your focus? It needs to be on the next play!"

Most coaches have shared the frustration that comes
from repeating something to an athlete who fails to
integrate it into his or her play. Coaches try many things,
but sometimes nothing seems to make it through. How can
coaches say things in a way that helps them to be heard?

Generally, when one gives feedback, one says too much.
Most of us are not trained in how to deliver feedback. We
are just expected to know how to do it. Giving feedback that
is critical of skills or behavior is one of the most challenging
forms of communication.

My experience watching coaches suggests that most
could do this more effectively. If there is one guiding
principle for delivery of feedback, it is *keep it short*. Brief,
concise feedback is something athletes regularly comment
that they need. It should also tell athletes *what* they are
doing wrong and instruct them in how to correct it. This
can be as simple as correcting their stance or adjusting their
arms or leg position. If at all possible, show the athletes what
they are supposed to be doing.

Obviously, every coach will get frustrated and angry at
times, and it is appropriate. The tone of your voice, however,
will greatly impact how well an athlete can take in the
information. If you are angry and frustrated, and the tone
of your voice is on edge or aggressive, you might not be
heard as well as when your tone is calm or businesslike.
This is because high emotional tone or stress may cause
some players to get defensive or go into a stress response

before they have actually heard what you have to say. I have watched the deflated expressions of players receiving harsh criticism from their coaches. Sometimes you can read their faces like a book. The downward look, the shame, the reddening of a face, these are all cues that let you know you have struck a chord of embarrassment or shame. When these states in the body are activated, we don't process things very well. Thus, your tone is critically important when delivering feedback. If you are in such a state that you cannot control your voice or tone, perhaps it is best to wait a little while to deliver the feedback. Even a three- to five-second pause and a deep breath can make a difference in the way that you speak to someone. It could allow you to be aware of the volume of your voice before speaking.

Now I have to add that not all athletes mind being yelled at in an aggressive way, but many do. I was once surprised by a basketball player's recall of his former coach yelling at him in a way that tore him apart. I asked him how he felt about it and whether it motivated him, and he said, "Oh, it was fine. Coach knows that I don't get off my butt until he yells at me." So occasionally you get athletes who have a thicker skin, or maybe they grew up with a parent who was a yeller. This is where it is critical to know the nuances of your players. A few will tell you that they need to be handled this way.

However, in studying some of the best coaches, we see the methodical, concise approach that is not overly emotional. John Wooden's coaching was analyzed for content after observations were done of his coaching in the 1970s. Gallimore and Tharp (2004) then analyzed it later. What they found was 50.3 percent of his communication was instructive. Interestingly, his communication was short and concise and spoken very quickly to his players. He did not need a lot of words to communicate instructions. The more words, the less likely the player will hear the message correctly. Several of Wooden's players report that his instructive feedback was what set him apart as a coach. Interestingly, even when Coach Wooden was "scolding" a player, he would do so in a manner that the researchers came to call "a Wooden." He would stop play with the whistle, demonstrate the correct way to perform the skill, then imitate the incorrect way the player had just done the skill, followed by the correct way once more (Gallimore and Tharp 2004). Coach Wooden called it a sandwich approach. Modeling the skill was key to his corrective feedback.

Another interesting strategy comes to us from Penn State University's Russ Rose, a four-time national coach of the year in women's volleyball. In a chapter written by sport psychologist David Yukelson, he describes the technique used by Coach Rose, calling it "the One-Minute Drill." At different times during the season, Coach Rose would pull aside a player for a one-minute meeting (individually, in the gym) and point out, "This is what I think you are doing well, this is what I think you need to work on, and here is where I see you making the best contribution to the team during the next training cycle" (Yukelson and Rose 2014). This type of short, direct feedback is to the point, honest, and in the moment. According to behavioral theory, reinforcement that follows a behavior close in time is the most effective in terms of getting the person to repeat the behavior. Timeliness is very important to feedback (both positive and negative), because players need to know what they are doing well and what needs work.

Coaching Reinforcement, Rules, and Feedback Tips

Reinforcement

- One of the most important aspects of reinforcement is that it should follow soon after the demonstration of a desirable behavior or skill. So if your team has done something well, or an athlete has completed a tough skill he or she has not done before, you want to react quickly. Positive reinforcement works best if it is right after the behavior.

- When athletes are younger or learning a skill, reinforce all correct movements. As they become more skilled, you can respond with praise sometimes in order to keep their efforts up. Reward effort to keep athletes working hard at all ages.

- Youth coaches are encouraged to use an 80:20 ratio of positive reinforcement to punishment ratio. Use punishment sparingly.

- Get to know your athletes in order to find out what they consider rewarding.

- Reinforce small steps in improvement on the way to mastering skills.

Rules

- Rules are most effective when they describe what an athlete is supposed to do (e.g., be at practice on time, dressed and ready, be respectful to coaches and teammates).

- Coaches need to enforce the rules consistently with all players. Starting players should not be excused from consequences of their actions on a team.
- If at all possible, involve players in coming up with some of the rules.

Feedback

- If there is one guiding principle for delivery of feedback, it is *keep it short*. Brief, concise feedback should tell athletes *what* they are doing wrong and instruct them in *how* to correct it. We do not need a lot of words to communicate instructions. The more words, the less likely the listener will hear the message correctly.
- Breathe a deep belly breath if you are angry or frustrated before you deliver the feedback.
- Coaches are human beings, and they can have bad days. When you are aware of yourself, you have choices or flexibility in how you respond.
- Try the one-minute meeting (individually, in the gym) and point out, "This is what I think you are doing well, this is what I think you need to work on, and here is where I see you making the best contribution to the team during the next training cycle."
- Alternatively, speak in a soft voice when giving feedback. This will shock your players if you are a loud coach, and it will increase their need to pay attention to hear you.

Chapter 3

MOTIVATION

"You all came really close in that game. Your passing and shooting was significantly better than last game. I also heard more talk out there between players. And despite coming in at the second half behind, you all rallied. I'm proud of your work and know that if we keep working the way we have been, perfecting our skills and working together, this team is going places!"

Versus:

"How could you lose to them? We beat them last year! You're better than them, but you couldn't tell last game. What were you thinking out there? Or were you thinking? After all the work we've done, I certainly expected a better outcome. You guys are going to be hurting today when I'm done with you."

As the receiver of these two messages, you would probably have completely different feelings and levels of motivation. The first message comes from a coach who believes in focusing on the development of skill in his or her players. The second is from a coach who is focused on outcome. With regard to motivation, an athlete doesn't have any control over a number of factors that affect outcome of competitions, such as how well prepared the other team is, the officials' calls during the competition, injuries to fellow players, and so on. However, with regard to themselves, players have a great deal of control. By appealing to the desires of athletes to get better at their sport and develop as individual and team players, coaches can build intrinsic motivation. Intrinsic motivation is an internal desire to become a better athlete due to an inherent enjoyment of the process and the game. Fundamentally, it is a love of the sport and an enjoyment of the growth process. Extrinsic motivation, on the other hand, is motivation that comes from outside of ourselves. It could be monetary, praise, prestige, or scholarships. It could be coaches' or parents' approval. The problem with extrinsic motivators is that these can lose their power to motivate. There are many discussions about college scholarships and the potential to negatively impact athlete motivation, because the sport becomes like a job.

Motivation is different from positive and negative reinforcement in that motivation has to do with harnessing energy to get something done. Reinforcement follows behavior; motivation precedes it. A coach's tendency to use positive versus negative communication in order to create belief will have a direct effect on athletes' levels of motivation. There are studies that demonstrate the impact of positive reinforcement on team morale and its indirect effect on motivation. This chapter will look at types of motivation, communication and its relationship to motivation, motivational transitions, and coaches' wellness and motivation.

Coach Mike Krzyewski, also known as Coach K, of Duke University basketball, shares his thoughts about his role as a coach in motivating his players:

> I believe that my work is as much about words as it is about basketball. Choosing the right words is no less important to the outcome of a game than choosing the right players and strategies for the court. As a coach, leader, and teacher, my primary task is motivation. How do I get a group motivated, not only to be their individual best, but also to become better as a team? I have always said that two are better than one, but only if two can act as one. (Krzyewski 2011)

Coach K insists that to motivate any team, you must know your audience. He tells the story of motivating Shane Battier after the 1999 season in which Duke lost the championship to Connecticut. He called this player during the off-season and asked him if when he got up that morning, he looked in the mirror and saw next year's conference player of the year. He proceeded to build in Shane Battier's mind his belief and expectations for his growth and role as a star of the team. Creating belief or painting a picture of success is motivating.

Another key aspect of motivation is communicating what you would like to see and harnessing players' energy to make it happen. It occurs at the thought level and the body level. It is about finding energy and direction to achieve a goal. In sport, there is individual motivation to work at goals, and there is team motivation to work hard to achieve desired outcomes. Coaches have a critical role in both. Mark Johnson, the former head baseball coach at Texas A&M University, never experienced a losing record on the collegiate level in twenty-five years. He also took his team to seven NCAA regional appearances. In the book *Competitive Excellence*, author Stephen Brennan interviewed Johnson. On motivation, Johnson stated: "To me, motivation is energetic movement. Much of that energy must be directed toward the commitment to goals." He added: "The players need to be self-motivated, as well. Your key players will be self-motivators."

Johnson developed several motivation techniques that he found to be helpful with his teams. One included always taking a *positive* approach with the players. He felt it set the tone for the program and kept things positive in dealing with both the team and individual players (Brennan 1995). His coaching staff worked hard to avoid using the words "not" and "don't" with the players. He also thought giving them positive and affirmative statements about what to do was helpful. In behavioral terms, this makes sense, because it is easier for individuals to see themselves doing something rather than *not* doing something. It also guides the brain to imagine or think of the *correct* movement. Additionally,

Johnson taught through pictures. The coaches visually demonstrated fundamental skills and concepts. Johnson thought that this emphasis removed the fear of failure that many athletes experience each day (Brennan 1995). Therefore, communicate in positive language that tells players what to do, and consider showing them the correct skills so that they can see what you want.

Intrinsic versus Extrinsic Motivation

One of the most important concepts in psychology that relates to motivation is that of intrinsic versus extrinsic motivation. The source of our motivation is *why* we do what we do. In simple terms, the difference between intrinsic and extrinsic motivation is that intrinsic motivation comes from within the athlete, and extrinsic motivation comes from external rewards. Research on self-determination theory (SDT) and motivation has shown that there are complex reasons people do things. The research has demonstrated that our reasons for doing something can change if you provide external rewards for an activity. This theory has also been applied to understanding motivation in sport (Ryan and Deci 2002). SDT looks at the continuum of reasons why people do what they do. On one end is the concept of *amotivation*, or having no internal or external reasons for participating in an activity (zero interest or energy). In the middle of the continuum are several types of extrinsic motivation, which describes how athletes are driven by a desire to receive outside rewards (e.g., trophies, cool uniforms). Another possibility in the middle of the continuum is athletes do what they do because they have taken in another person's reasons (e.g., parents) for participation, reasons that are tied to internal rewards and punishments.

Thus, an athlete can play for many different reasons. Some examples of external reasons are status, pleasing parents, or monetary gains like scholarships or hopes of a future professional career. Optimally, coaches would love athletes to be intrinsically motivated, or choosing the activity freely and because they love to engage in the sport. Studies have shown that the higher the level of self-directed motivation, the higher the level of task perseverance and psychological well-being (Gagne, Ryan, and Bargmann 2003). This means that an athlete who is playing for his or her own reasons will work harder to achieve their goals. They also found that those who are autonomously motivated reported lower levels of feelings of stress, anxiety, and self-criticism in sport (Gagne, Ryan, and Bargmann 2003). To summarize then, an athlete who plays because he or she loves the game experiences less stress than one who is playing for someone or something other than himself or herself.

The danger of athletic scholarships, in terms of motivation, is that we make the reasons for being engaged in the sport different from what they may have been previously. The source of the reward is no longer within the individual and is now external and financial (e.g., college tuition, board, and fees). This can change incentives for playing from love of the game to attempts to please the coach in order to have their scholarships renewed. This is simply a reality of college-level sports, but it does change the nature of the incentives to play.

Although most high school athletes are not playing for scholarship money, many play on club or travel teams, which can create threats to intrinsic motivation or playing for love of the game. External rewards for playing on a competitive travel team may include fancy uniforms, high status among peers, and trophies. Pleasing parents is another frequently cited reason why an athlete plays a sport. I have been surprised by the number of college athletes who were coached by one of their parents at some point in their athletic career. I once asked a women's collegiate Division I team how many of them had a parent as a coach. Almost every hand in the room was raised!

One of the key factors affecting motivation is self-determination. Self-determination means that the athlete is freely choosing his or her sport and it is within his or her control. All of us, according to the theory of SDT, need to feel competent, autonomous, and connected to others. If athletes have chosen to pursue a sport for their own reasons, and they feel competent at their sport and connected to teammates, the athletes will have a greater sense of well-being. In high school, most athletes choose to play their sport, but many have the goal of playing at the college level. This is highly competitive and takes a great deal of work and perseverance to achieve. Thus, even high school students must remain connected to their own reasons for playing a sport, because parents may be invested in their getting a scholarship to college, which is an extrinsic motivator. This can interfere with the athlete's inherent desire to play the sport.

Motivational Transitions

Many college athletes enter their freshman year excited and motivated to play. However, often they lose steam because they are no longer the best player on their team, and they may warm the bench quite a bit. They may also come to feel that their sport is more like a job with their coach as the boss. Their reasons for playing their beloved sport begin to change. They also move away from parents, who are often a huge source of emotional support in their athletic life. The feeling of *having* to engage in the practices and games may also cause them to lose their love of the game.

Human beings generally like to feel in control, and this is especially true of young adults, including older high school and college-aged athletes. Western society supports the development of independence as an adolescent gets older. In most families in the United States, it is a normal for teens to push off from the family and move toward friends, especially as a teen gets older. Often, athletes who are good enough to play in college have spent quite a bit of time playing in high school, on travel or club teams, and for their schools. As they shift to the typical Division I athlete's schedule, it is packed with practices, weight training, team meetings, and, during the season, travel to games. Often, the entire travel weekend is scheduled—from breakfast to practice to study hall time. Young adult athletes' natural desire to be in charge of their own lives may be negatively impacted by their participation on a college team. Some of them have a hard time when they are not allowed to have influence over the scheduling of their lives on a day-to-day basis. This can remove the sense that their involvement in the sport is voluntary. The commitment to hard work and dedication to training is critical. Thus, the coach's ability to motivate and inspire his or her players is essential. The aforementioned research on the importance of free choice to motivation suggests that good coaches might allow some control or choice to their athletes. This relates back to our discussion in chapter 1 of the relationship between parenting styles and coaching. The authoritative coach who balances between responsiveness and high demands yet maintains some control would offer these types of choices. How might coaches do this? They might allow athletes to choose workouts, offer choices between the drills they do, and give some freedom to athletes in their day-to-day life. They might let an athlete plan a practice. If the athletes feel their input is valued, they will be more committed to the process. Obviously, the coach wants his or her athletes to value team over individual wants, but an occasional allowance of this type of freedom might bring some interesting results.

Wellness and Motivation

Another aspect of being an excellent motivator is that you, as a coach, take good care of yourself. You are the leader of your team. Obviously, everyone has a bad day sometimes, and we all lose our patience sometimes. But *your* psychological well-being and energy contribute to the emotional climate on your team.

If you are struggling in some area of your life, you may need to do some extra work to care for yourself. Hopefully, coaching brings you joy. But it is also an emotionally demanding job. Caring for your team is sometimes like having another family. Finding the right words, disciplining members when they step out of line, inspiring the players toward excellence, supporting them after losses amidst your own disappointments and pressures from your bosses—all of this requires personal energy. Most of us get into coaching because we love the game and dealing with young athletes. Being aware of yourself as the instrument of your trade and caring well for yourself when you are exhausted or stressed is important. Obviously, certain personal practices like exercise, prayer or meditation, a sense of purpose or mission, and the support of family are critical to one's well-being. Self-care can help you remain balanced and energized as a coach.

Coaching Tips on Motivation

Get to know your players as individuals and as a team. Why do they play? What do they love about their sport? What inspires them to work hard? What are their goals for themselves and as a team?

- Articulate your goals for the team clearly and frequently. Post them in the locker room. Set goals for practice as a way of focusing their efforts.
- Tell stories of players or individuals from your life who inspire you or who work very hard at their goals.
- State your goals for players in positive terms, meaning the goal should tell them *what* to do, not what *not* to do.
- Try to offer older adolescent athletes some choices in choosing workouts, such as which drill to

practice first, or any other small choices within the framework of practice or training. Try to make it fun by offering variety. Let them choose their clothing for practice (if practice uniforms are required, use this as a special benefit on occasion).

- Pick a fun or goofy practice activity and let the players blow off some steam and laugh. It's good for them, and then when you ask them to get back to work, they will feel like they have had a break.

- Mind your energy so that you can inspire their energy and keep it high. If you come to practice with a sense of drudgery, you probably will not inspire your players to work hard. Your attitude and energy are contagious!

Chapter 4

GOAL SETTING

Last year, I was talking to a coach of a Division I softball team at a holiday gathering. He was lamenting the fact that many of his players would go home for the break and lose the traction they had gained in practice and the weight room over the past months. In talking to his assistant coaches, I asked them if they had the players set goals for the break. They said, "No, we hadn't really thought about that." One of the outcomes of our conversation was for them to ask each player to articulate a goal for the holiday break. I reviewed the goals, and many of them were quite vague. For example, "I want to improve my hitting." The player was asked to refine this into some kind of practice or action. She came back with, "I will take a hundred cuts per day. I will hit at the batting cages twice a week." This was precisely what the coaches wanted, as the player would know whether she did this or not, and she could keep track of it. They also set up a text system, whereby the player would text one of the coaches each week to let him or her know how he or she was on their goals.

One of the most common psychological skills used by high performers is that they set goals. Goal setting has been clearly demonstrated in the psychological research to help with task performance (Locke et al. 1981). Studies of Olympic and elite athletes have consistently shown that they set goals, monitor progress, and reevaluate (Weinberg et al. 2000). The theory of goal setting has been researched in business and has been primarily developed by Dr. Edwin Locke, who began goal-setting research in the 1960s. The research demonstrated a relationship between goal setting and improved production performance. A goal is the aim of an action or task that a person consciously desires to achieve (Locke and Latham 2002). Goals have a pervasive influence on employee behavior and performance in organizations and management practice (Locke and Latham 2002). Nearly every modern organization has some form of goal setting in operation (Lunenburg 2011).

Goals help us by focusing our energies and actions in desired directions. Working with people on behavioral changes in my practice, I have found that focusing on goals is one of the critical elements to mobilize effort. This chapter will discuss different ways of setting goals, types of goals, and what the research tells us about goal setting and performance.

When thinking about achievement-oriented goals, experts distinguish between *task goals* (also called process goals or mastery) and *outcome goals*. Task goals have to do with skills, whereas outcome goals have to do with winning. Task goals are oriented toward mastery or getting better at a skill, and outcome goals are related to winning or success in competition. Some examples of task goals are a volleyball player who would like to reach a higher hitting percentage, a baseball or softball player who wants to increase his or her batting average, or a basketball player who wants to increase his or her free-throw percentage.

Goals should be SMART: specific, measurable, action oriented, realistic, timely, and self-determined (Weinberg and Butt 2010). Self-determined means they are freely chosen and committed to by the person setting the goal. Goals also tell us what to do. They should specify in positive terms what an athlete will do. For example, during the winter break, some athletes set fitness and training goals. Some of them wanted to improve their cardio; others wanted to get stronger in the weight room. Their coach wanted to know what they planned to *do*. How often would they do cardio or go to the weight room? What times would they try to make? Or, for weight training, were they looking to maintain or improve their strength? By how much? If they wanted to improve their diet, what changes would they make (e.g., eat less sugar, increase protein intake, etc.)? The more specific the goal, the easier it is to figure out if you are achieving it or not. Asking athletes how committed they are to their goal is another important question. Also, who can help you reach this goal?

Another useful part of motivating a team, whether business or athletic, is the *why* of the goal. Communicating why we are trying to reach the goal can help to generate focused effort. Simon Sinek, a leadership expert, says that people need to know not just the *what* and how of reaching goals but the *why.* He says great leaders connect their teams to the *why* of the goal. History has shown us that great leaders (and great coaches) are first and foremost great communicators. An acquaintance of mine who is a CEO of a large hospital network said that he believes strong leaders tell stories to connect with their employees and teams. If we cannot effectively convey to our athletes why a goal is important, we won't be as effective in persuading them to use this tool. Obviously, teams want to win championships. But coaches hope to motivate players to become better at their sport and to become great teammates and leaders as well.

As a coach, you can use reinforcement or rewards as your team reaches some of their task goals, in order to support continued effort and hard work. For example, your basketball team has trouble with free-throw scoring; if the team reaches a 65 percent success rate on free-throw shots, you will reward them with something celebratory (e.g., a day off from practice, food, or an outing). This can help players feel successful even if they are not yet winning.

Realistic Goal Setting

Many times, athletes or individuals set goals that are too difficult. This does not mean that we don't encourage people to shoot high. It means that the goal needs to be realistic and attainable. For example, losing ten pounds in a week is not reasonable. It can be done, but the weight will likely be regained quickly. It is much more attainable to set a goal of a pound or two a week. Although this will not bring about instant change, it will result in a gradual shift without drastically changing behavior in a way that could be harmful. In the same way, setting skills goals (e.g., improving my free-throw percentage by 5 percent in a month or two) is an attainable goal with practice and commitment. Articulating what action steps a player will take might include adding one hundred free throws a day to the practice schedule and computing the free-throw percentage each week to monitor improvement.

In my sport psychology classes, students conduct a final project in which they have to work with an athlete on a physical skill or training goal over the course of six to eight weeks. Quite often, the chosen athlete will set a goal that is too ambitious, and the student "consultant" unknowingly agrees. When the athlete does not make progress, I often suggest that the student consultant revise the goal. An example is an athlete who wants to cut a certain time off of his forty-yard sprint. If the athlete wanted to cut speed by a half a second, and the athlete was already quite fast, the goal was unrealistic. Shaving time off of an already fast performance is harder. Most progress in athletic goals is made over time, in small increments. When athletes do not reach a goal because it is too difficult, they can become discouraged and easily shift to the faulty belief that they cannot improve in the skill. Instead, setting small short-term goals and reaching them from week to week, the athlete ends up reaching the long-term goal over time.

Another key point in helping an athlete to set goals is making sure he or she doesn't set too many goals at once. People have a hard time focusing on more than one thing at a time, and this is even truer when they are under stress. Thus, asking players to focus on one goal—or maybe two—at a time is plenty. Once the goals are reached, new goals can be set. Team goals can also be set, but groups probably struggle in the same way as individuals, so focus your team on no more than one or two goals at a time.

Self-determination of goals is also important. This means that the athlete chooses the goal and is committed to it. We don't tend to work hard in the direction of things that aren't important to us. We will, however, exert much effort toward goals we want badly. Gardner and Moore (2007) have incorporated this idea into their training to improve human performance. Early on in the program, they have athletes determine what their performance values are and then formulate their goals with those values in mind. If you want to be a better teammate, what does that mean in terms of behaviors? Anchoring goals to specific behaviors is critical, because goals tell us what to do. Being a better teammate may be achieved by making five positive statements to my teammates during practice, getting together for a meal outside of practice on a regular basis, or encouraging my teammates during competition.

Short-Term and Long-Term Goals

Research by Weinberg (2010) suggests that coaches and athletes set both short-term and long-term goals. An example of a short-term training goal would be to get to the weight room three days a week and do three sets of ten reps on the weights. An example of a long-term goal would be to bench-press thirty additional pounds at the end of four months. That breaks down the additional weight pressed to 7.5 pounds per month. Divided by four weeks per month, that is just under two pounds a week. An athlete might feel intimidated by thirty additional pounds at the outset, but when he or she thinks about 1.85 pounds a week, he or she will feel it is more doable. Short-term goals mobilize our energy and focus our actions.

Practice and Competition Goals

Athletes also need to set practice and competition goals. It is helpful to write down goals and record or monitor changes or progress. Cell phone technology can assist with reporting and keeping track of goals. There are several apps available: Smart Goals, Goals on Track, Lift, and Optimize Me are a few examples. These are all possible ways of monitoring progress using goal setting in order to improve performance. However, I believe that telling our coach or a teammate about our goal and being accountable keeps us honest in a way that a cell phone app cannot. Coaches can also help their team focus during practice by setting goals for the practice sessions or for the week. For example, a soccer team that performed poorly on corner kicks in the last game can focus the following week's practice sessions on improving the corner kicks.

Goals in Positive Terms

When articulating particular goals, an athlete should describe behaviors or skills in positive terms. For example, a hockey player stating that he or she will stay out of the penalty box may be the outcome wished for, but stating it in those terms does not tell the athlete what he or she needs to do. Instead, they might state the goal in terms of keeping their head cool, taking deep breaths when aggravated or frustrated, and choosing to respond without laying hands on a player or yelling at an official. Directing the athlete's focus to the desired behaviors rather than the behaviors to be avoided helps the athlete keep the positive goal in mind. Monitoring the progress on this goal means keeping track of the total penalty minutes in each game.

Measurement of Goals

Measurement is critical when setting goals. This is one of the most frequent errors people make when setting a goal. They say they want to get in shape or get stronger or faster. What does it mean, and how will it be measured? Simply put, will getting in shape mean they can bench-press more weight (if so, how much?), or will it mean losing weight (how much weight, over what period of time?), or does it mean getting faster and trimming five seconds off their personal best in a race? Obviously, behavioral goals must be measurable; otherwise we will not know if we have met the goal. Specific goals are thought to regulate action better than general goals (Locke and Latham 1985).

Another suggestion by Locke and Latham, who wrote about applying goal setting to sports (Locke and Latham 1985), is to create a point system because it allows performance measurement. An individual is given a certain number of points for each accomplishment during a game or competition. In this way, goals can be set in terms of attaining a certain number of points in a specific time period. An example of this would be a basketball coach giving a point for every free-throw shot made or every rebound made. In baseball or softball, a pitcher could gain points for every strike thrown or strike out. A fielder might get points for every catch or throw in to base done correctly.

Some of my sport psychology students have worked with basketball players on their projects. They will often use reinforcers to help their athletes progress on their free-throw shots. A favorite reinforcer is a meal pass, because athletes are often hungry! When they reach a goal of taking a certain number of shots successfully, at the end of the week they are given a free meal. Interestingly, the athletes have often responded well. Is it practice effects? Is it moving in the direction of a goal? Is it the extra incentive of trying to get the desired free meal? It's probably a combination of the three, but it works!

One of the more challenging goals that coaches might have for their teams is greater communication. One of the most recognizable differences in this generation of college students (and the rest of us!) is that we are often plugged in, meaning looking at our phones, ear buds in, or listening to music. Coaches have shared with me that athletes don't always talk to each other on the bus trips to competitions. Some of that informal communication adds to a deeper knowledge of teammates, as well as a comfort with them. So if a goal is to communicate more, specify when—during practice, en route to games, or during competition. Give your athletes questions that they need to ask to learn about each other.

Coaching Tips on Setting Goals

Individually

- Encourage athletes to set task goals for practice and goals for competition.
- Set SMART goals: specific, measurable, action oriented, realistic, timely, and self-determined.
- Be sure that they (or the coaching staff) keep track of their goals.
- Have players set short-term and long-term task goals and track them.
- Ask how important this goal is to the athlete. If it is not important to him or her, have him or her set another goal.
- Check in periodically and give feedback to players about how they are doing on their individual goals.
- Limit goals to one or two at a time, as people cannot focus on too many goals at once.
- Set age-appropriate goals; for example, young kids are working at a more fundamental level, and that is okay. Older athletes are refining skills.

Team

- Let the team know what your task and outcome goals are for them as a group (e.g., improving their level of play, winning a certain percentage of games, improving a particular statistic such as the number of penalty kicks or a free-throw percentage, improving fitness levels such as speed or strength in the weight room, or making it to a tournament).
- Write down these goals and post them in the locker room—visual cues help us stay mindful of our goals.
- Ask the team what their hopes are for the season. If they are vague, ask for more specifics.
- Ask them how important it is to them to reach these team goals and *why*.
- Consider rewarding athletes in some way when they reach task and outcome goals (short-term and long-term).
- Translate team goals into what the team will *do* in practice to make this happen.
- Remind the team of their team goals on a regular basis.

Chapter 5

SELF-EFFICACY AND CONFIDENCE

A coach to his team at halftime: "You've done this a million times in practice, and I know you can pull this off! All we have to do is play the game we know how to play and have been playing for the past few weeks. You're capable—let's do it!"

A coach speaks to her athlete in practice: "Stephanie, you have the ability to do this move on the beam. You've practiced it hundreds of times on the floor and on the low beam. The beam is the same width up high that it is down low. See yourself doing this—imagine you're up there, and you're so comfortable because it's second nature. See your body moving in space. Feel the motion as your legs rotate through the tuck. I know you can do this!"

The power of verbal persuasion is something we've all witnessed in sports. The intense gaze of a coach as he or she talks to the athlete before competition, the convincing tone of a coach's voice as the team listens at halftime, the energy coaches infuse. Coaches help to create belief and confidence in an athlete's ability to do his or her sport, to master difficult skills, and to compete at a high level. As we will see, verbal persuasion is just one of the major influences on a person's self-efficacy, or their belief in their ability to do something specific. These beliefs are not competencies; they are *beliefs about* one's competencies. What is vital to realize as a coach is that beliefs shape our behaviors and expectations, and a critical skill in coaching is creating belief.

We have areas of self-efficacy about all kinds of abilities in our life. For example, we have self-efficacy about our driving, about how regular an exerciser we are, about our ability to speak in front of a large group of people or ask someone out on a date. Thus, the beliefs are connected to situations; they are our beliefs about our skills and abilities under certain conditions. In sports, we also have self-efficacy. A quarterback has beliefs about his ability to make certain plays successfully, and a pitcher has a set of beliefs about his or her ability to strike batters out. Teams also have a collective efficacy about their ability to compete and win. Albert Bandura, the psychologist who came up with the concept of self-efficacy, believed that people's level of motivation, emotional states, and actions are based more on what they *believe* than what is *objectively true* (Bandura 1997). This is an incredible statement. It speaks to the power of belief and coaching. Coaches who believe in their athletes and their team's ability to do something communicate this powerfully at critical moments—pregame, halftime, between matches or sets, and so on. A coach's energy and belief *and* his or her ability to transmit that to a team are vital to the life of the team. There are a number of ways to increase self-efficacy. The next section explores the critical factors.

Factors in Self-Efficacy

Simply put, our beliefs shape our behaviors. Bandura said there are four main influences on self-efficacy:

- An athlete's performance experiences and thoughts about the results of his or her past performance experiences. Outcomes that are interpreted as successful raise self-efficacy; those interpreted as failures lower it.

  So whether an athlete thinks he or she was successful (or not) in his or her past performance will influence how he or she feels about the next game. Also, if an athlete has done something before in practice and believes he or she can do it again, he or she is more likely to successfully perform it in competition.

- Vicarious experiences and particularly modeling: this is all about watching someone do something. If the model or player is very much like the athlete, then the impact of their example is even stronger.

  Pairing an athlete with someone like himself or herself who is more skilled or experienced can be helpful. If they like the person and relate to him or her, even better! This may also be meaningful if the person has similar physical attributes. We look up to those who we want to be like and who have abilities we would like to have.

Assigning athletes a buddy on a team can help them transition onto the team. It can also generate trust among players, as well as let new teammates know what is going on. Plus it gives ample opportunities for modeling.

- The result of social persuasion: people develop self-beliefs through listening to the spoken judgments of others. Parents, friends, and former coaches have a great deal of influence; persuasive people in an athlete's life (and those they trust) can increase their belief in their abilities. However, this must be somewhat reality based. A coach or parent should be able see the potential *and* the accompanying practice and hard work in order to say to the athlete, "You can do X." Just telling an athlete he or she can do something without the athlete having put in the practice is not based on reality.

  Note: It is easier to weaken one's beliefs through negative appraisals than to strengthen beliefs through positive encouragement. What that means is that the negative things you say to an athlete or a team about their *inability* to do something stick in their minds and are possibly more influential than encouragement (Bandura 1997). Beware of heavy criticism!

- Somatic/emotional states: anxiety, stress, arousal, and mood states influence efficacy beliefs. People can gauge their degree of confidence by the emotional state they experience as they contemplate an action. One way to raise self-efficacy beliefs is to improve physical and emotional well-being and reduce negative emotional states. Athletes are more likely to doubt their competence in unpleasant physical states of arousal than when they are less aroused. By arousal, I mean the degree of physiological activation in the body, not arousal in the sexual sense, which is the more popular use of the word. People judge their fatigue, aches, and pains as signs of physical debility; mood also impacts this. However, athletes can play well even if they don't feel perfectly well, if they remain focused and trust themselves and their experience.

Mindfulness practice can help athletes accept negative feeling states as part and parcel of athletic life. As a reminder, mindfulness is about being fully aware in the present moment, without filters or the lens of judgment (Stahl and Goldstein 2010). Using mindfulness exercises can help athletes accept their fatigue or bodily states and get into the present moment with a more external focus and attention on the relevant cues. Pausing for short periods of time, as George Mumford has done with the Lakers and the Knicks, pregame or at halftime, can be like a reset button. See chapter 7, "Arousal and Anxiety," for examples of these mindfulness practices.

Self-Efficacy Affects Our View of Challenges

People who have been shown to have high levels of self-efficacy (confidence or belief in their power to do something particular) do not shy away from difficult or challenging tasks or see them as threatening but instead believe they can exercise control over them. They also tend to visualize successful scenarios because they believe they can happen. And lastly, they view failures as due to insufficient effort rather than low ability. Think about that last statement. Wouldn't you rather have your athletes thinking that they just need to work harder after a failure than to think that they will never win a game?

Collective efficacy comes about when a group is successful together. Playing hard together, facing adversity in games or competition, succeeding under pressure, or just playing their hearts out together can build collective efficacy. This also generates a level of trust in each other as fellow athletes.

Another technique from sport psychology that has been used to teach and build confidence is self-talk. This will be discussed in the next section.

Self-Talk

A technique used by high-level athletes that coaches can teach is called self-talk. What is self-talk? An internal dialogue or chatter that is almost always unknown to the individual because it is so automatic. We have thousands of thoughts a day, but often, unless you specifically ask people to focus on their thoughts and report them back to you, they may be unaware of the negative aspects to their thinking. Self-talk is an asset when it enhances self-worth and performance, and it can also be a drawback if it is negative and creates doubt.

Gould, Eklund, and Jackson (1992a, 1992b) studied Olympic wrestlers and showed that self-talk was a technique that wrestlers used to foster positive expectancies and to help focus attention. They also said they had more positive expectancy and task-specific self-talk (thoughts about what to do) before their best versus their worst performances. However, there is mixed evidence on this. One review (Tod, Hardy, and Oliver 2011) did not find evidence that negative self-talk impeded performance. There is much qualitative research on athletes, though, that suggests that negative self-talk can hurt performance. Athletes using self-talk interventions have shown improvement, and college and national team coaches ranked encouraging, positive self-talk as the third most important factor for confidence after (1) practice and (2) modeling confidence (Gould et al. 1989). Keeping a self-talk log can be very helpful to increase awareness of thoughts. In particular, keeping a log helps athletes become aware of situations that prompt negative self-talk and the consequences of it. It can also give them an opportunity to try to replace negative thoughts with positive, affirming statements.

In my sport psychology classes, students do case studies with athletes working on a behavioral change. These studies have shown changing self-talk to be effective for a number of individuals. The science on self-talk is mixed, but for some athletes, tuning into their negative self-talk can be an eye-opening experience and a powerful way to try to change their thinking.

Coaches influence self-talk. Athletes exposed to supportive coaching behaviors had more positive self-talk; athletes exposed to negative coaching behaviors had more negative self-talk (Zourbanos et al. 2010). Negative self-talk affects how we feel about ourselves. We know that people who suffer from depression and anxiety tend to have negative thoughts about themselves, their futures, and the world (Beck et al. 1979). Before a competition, athletes have many anticipatory thoughts. Keeping these positive can build confidence.

There is some evidence that more self-talk occurs in competition than at practice (Hardy, Hall, and Hardy 2005). Some athletes have an affirming phrase that directs their approach. For example, when serving the ball in tennis or taking a penalty kick, one may say to oneself, "Top left corner of the net," or, "Back corner of the court." What is interesting is that athletes in individual sports and more-skilled athletes use positive self-talk more often than athletes in team sports and less-skilled athletes. Obviously, personal pressure runs higher in individual sports like golf, gymnastics, tennis, and diving. All eyes are on the individual athlete, and there is no hiding when he or she screws up. As a result, the thinking that precedes performance is important.

Sometimes self-talk is used to control or increase effort or motivation. Cues can enhance performance; runners who say, "Fast," or, "Quick," have been found to increase their speed. Or coming out of the blocks, a sprinter says, "Explode!" Motivational self-talk is also good for energizing and helping to maximize effort. "Come on! Go all out!" Emphasizing effort is helpful because it keeps an athlete focused on hard work.

Self-talk can also be used to change or reinterpret what's going on in the body or mind before competition as not problematic. For example, nerves or the jitters before competition could be a sign of excitement rather than anxiety. Hanton and Jones (1999) found that competitive swimmers who perceived their precompetition anxiety as a problem could be taught to use self-talk to reinterpret the anxiety as helpful (excitement). This has also has been done with golfers.

Coaching Tips on Self-Efficacy and Confidence

- Communicate belief in your athletes' abilities as individuals and as a group. Make sure they hear and believe what you say. It is important to be honest. If you don't believe your team can win yet, you should emphasize the notion that they are gaining in competence and, with continued work and effort, *will* win. But you must be persuasive! Inspire hard work with your belief in your team or athlete. Tell them what you think they need to do to be competitive.
- Veer away from harsh criticism. Athletes remember negative things said by coaches for a long time; they are like flypaper for negative remarks. Negative comments stay with us and can erode our good beliefs about ourselves. Choose your words wisely. If you are upset and tend to lay into the team in ways that are not helpful, take a break and deliver feedback later when you have better control.

- Halftime is a prime opportunity to communicate faith in a team. Constructive language that emphasizes what you believe is possible is key.
- Visualization exercises that help the team to see themselves as individuals or as a group performing perfectly can be helpful to create belief. This involves forethought.
- Mindfulness exercises can return a team's focus to the present moment and help them to hit a reset button mentally. It can also help athletes who are in a negative emotional space to shift out of it. Teach mindfulness activities before practice and even clearing breaths during practice and games. See chapter 7, "Arousal and Anxiety," for scripts. This helps athletes to recognize what a clear mind and relaxed body feels like.
- Emphasize to a team that they have done this skill a thousand times in practice; they know how to do it and simply have to do what they already know how to do.
- Suggest to athletes that have a lot of issues with self-doubt or anxiety that they keep a self-talk log to see what and when they tend to go negative in their heads. Suggest brief phrases or cue words to help them refocus their energy and effort. Use phrases like these:
  o Trust yourself.
  o Nice and easy.
  o You've got this.
  o Explode (for burst activities).
  o Smooth (for finesse movements).
  o High and inside (pitcher).

- Have athletes reflect on their poor performance in helpful ways, not with heavy self-criticism but with an eye toward what they can do in the next performance situation to correct an error. Emphasize effort and working toward improvement. This increases motivation.

- Have athletes choose their own performance phrases based on their own ideas about how they need to move. The Russian sport psychologist Y. L. Hanin developed the idea of an individualized zone of optimal functioning (meaning performance). He explored the best emotional states that helped performance for athletes in different sports. Obviously, ice hockey players need different emotional states to play well compared to ice skaters or gymnasts. From this, Hanin and his colleagues had athletes come up with metaphors that described their readiness for action (e.g., a tiger ready to pounce, a well-working pipeline) (Hanin 2000c).

Chapter 6

TEAM COHESION

It is an ordinary practice day, and your team has assembled in the gym. After warm-ups, you decide to start the practice with scrimmage time and divide the group in two. One of the guys who is always a highly energetic player is just not with it. He looks like he didn't sleep last night. He also doesn't seem to be talking to his teammates. Something's off. You watch more closely and notice that he is not passing the ball to one of the other players he usually favors. What's up? You decide to change things up after a few minutes. "Let's practice a drill." They're still dead. Unbelievably quiet. What's going on? Something has shifted since the game two days ago, and they're not operating as a group at all. What to do?

The above scenario is not atypical for many teams. Teams are composed of people, and people are always changing. Often, things transpire on and off the court that influence how well teammates mesh and play together. But as a coach, you are often the last to know the latest drama. You just get to deal with the results. This is especially true if you are relatively new to the group or if you tend to keep a more formal relationship between you and your players. How well the team gets along can have a huge impact on play, so you can't just ignore it. But do you address the players directly when you know something is going on? Or do you pull a player aside and ask? Or do you ask the team captains? Will they tell you? It all depends on the issue and the level of trust they feel with you as their coach. This chapter will try to explain what cohesion is, along with some of the factors that influence team cohesion, and then suggest some specific activities that you can implement to increase a sense of bonding within the team.

Cohesion Dynamics

Carron and his colleagues defined cohesion as "a dynamic process which is reflected in the tendency for a group to stick together and remain united in the pursuit of its instrumental objectives [goals] and/or for the satisfaction of member affective [emotional] needs" (Carron, Brawley, and Widmeyer 1998). In other words, cohesion is how well a group works together toward its goals or purpose (Carron, Brawley, and Widmeyer 1998). I like to think of cohesion as the emotional glue that holds people together. Groups can work toward certain tasks (e.g., improving their defense) or they can work toward operating more effectively as a unit in order to win games. Widmeyer, Carron, and Brawley (1993) did a review of the research and found that 83 percent of studies reported a positive relationship between cohesion and performance.

Every player on a team has a different and unique bond to the team. Each player has his or her own read on how close or tight the team is. This is based on how much he or she likes working with their team, how much he or she enjoys their sport, and their connection to the group socially. Cohesion has been divided into two main types: task cohesion, or the degree to which an athlete sticks to the task at hand, and social cohesion, or the social bond to the group.

Task Cohesion

Task cohesion refers to the degree to which members of a group or team work together to achieve common goals, such as winning a game or a match. One athlete in my class defined it as "being of one mind." How hard a group works in practice and in competition is reflective of their task cohesion. Working together on skills and drills or plays can help to foster task cohesion. In addition, when team members encourage the group to work hard together on a specific task, they are creating a greater sense of task cohesion. Task-oriented coaching (which focuses on the development of skills) has been differentiated from ego-oriented coaching (focused on outcomes or winning) in the literature. A task-focused coach helps to develop intrinsic drive in his or her team members to work to be the best in their skill area.

Social Cohesion

Social cohesion, on the other hand, is the degree to which members of a team like each other and are attracted or bonded with the group. Athletes will tend to get together and socialize with teammates that they like and enjoy spending time with. All teams have subgroups due their likes and dislikes, their year in school, backgrounds, and so on (Janssen 1999). What can be difficult is when cliques form. "A clique occurs when a group of players set themselves off from the team and feel they are somehow better than certain teammates" (Janssen 1999). The trouble with this situation is that a fractioned team can negatively affect communication. It also can communicate disrespect, which erodes cohesion. Coaches need to communicate and model the value of respecting all members of the team, as well as assistant coaches, regardless of personal liking. At times, they need to confront situations that affect how well the group communicates and works as a team. Sometimes players will deal with one another directly when there are issues or disagreements within the group. I have seen teams choose to meet alone, without their coaches, to confront one another about a problem. This is ideal because it helps them work out their issues together and should not necessarily involve you as a coach.

> Respect is essential to building group cohesion. People who do not respect others

will not make good team members, and they probably lack self-esteem themselves. You don't have to like each other. But you do have to respect your colleagues' opinions and decisions, because your personal success depends on commitment to the overall plan and doing your part to make it work.

—Pat Summitt, University of Tennessee women's basketball (1998)

Cohesion Factors

There are a number of factors that contribute to team cohesion. Some of them are controllable, and some you have less influence over as a coach. This section will discuss some of the factors in detail.

Proximity, or how closely the players live to one another, makes a difference in how bonded they are as a group (Carron and Eys 2012). Many college teams have their players live together or next to each other in university housing. Having close contact means they will interact and communicate more often. The team members also spend hours and hours together at practice, in the weight room, and in competition. Often when they travel, they share all meals together, and they have little time to themselves. Thus, the nature of most college-level teams is such that there is a great deal of closeness. For high school teams, this is much different. Players come from different neighborhoods, and they don't necessarily have much contact outside of team practices or games. Thus, coaches may need to plan outside activities in the beginning of the season to help players get to know each other. They can also use short icebreaker-type activities to expose players to each other. Most college coaches plan group activities or team-building games early in the season, since each year there are new freshmen or transfer players. Simply increasing the amount of time and social contact a group has can build cohesion.

When players understand and accept their roles on the team, this can also help a team play well as a group (Beauchamp et al. 2002). A coach can make these roles known to the players as individuals early in the season. It is important for players to know how they will be evaluated and what will lead to successful fulfillment of their role (e.g., for a pitcher in baseball or softball, what stats should they hit in terms of performance). Players also benefit from knowing what will happen if they don't fulfill their roles (e.g., less playing time or not starting). Coaches can express the value of all members of the team, not just the starters. Recognizing different players' contributions verbally can affirm players and help them to feel satisfied that they are making a difference, even if it is small. Some coaches have rotated captains during the season to provide for a shared sense of responsibility. Others make a point to draw attention to the accomplishments of players who are being developed to play a larger role in the coming years. This building up of individual players, and emphasis on improvement over time, will earn lots of points toward improving the bond that players feel to the team and their overall cohesion as a group.

Another aspect that contributes to group cohesion is shared adversity (Janssen 1999). Players or people who go through difficulty together tend to bond. Military units who have weathered training or combat together tend to bond tightly. Friends who go through the birth of a child together and share the challenges of the baby's first year tend to bond. Anything that is tough on the body or the mind can create a strong connection between those who endure it together. Part of what makes winning teams and tough teams is how they deal with adversity. Mental toughness depends upon the leadership of coaches—as well as key team members—who persuade the team to stay tough when they begin to confront obstacles, such as losing a lead, errors, bad calls from the referees, trash-talking from the opponents, an unexpected injury of a teammate, or a player getting pulled from the game.

Helping a team practice some of these scenarios can build strategies for dealing with them in competition. Adding levels of pressure or intensity to make things harder at practice can also build toughness with adversity. Think of Bikram (hot) yoga, where the temperature of the room is about 105 degrees. Yoga is considered by most people to be a gentle form of exercise, but going through the poses in that heat increases the heart rate, causes intense sweating, and makes the whole workout more challenging. How can you, as a coach, help your team go through adversity together? Can you intensify practices such that they build toughness?

Team Norms

Team norms are another factor that contributes to group cohesion. Coaches must establish standards for how they expect their players to act and let them know what will happen if they do not. For example, something as simple as being late to practice or not showing up for practice will have consequences. Involving all of your team members in forming group rules and standards of conduct can help improve their sticking to those rules. Rewarding team members who adhere to these rules is important, and delivering consequences to those who do not is key in terms of follow-through. Something you have to consider as a coach is, do you penalize the whole team for one person's mistake? Although I don't think this makes sense for all situations, it may be important for some situations, when the individual's mistake has a huge effect on the team.

One coach I know asked team members to independently coming up with the most important values on the team. The coaching staff then put them together and isolated the top four values that players prized most. These were then discussed and displayed in the locker room. Players were asked to memorize and know the essential values of their team.

A recent study that considered touch, cooperation, and performance in the NBA has interesting implications for coaches (Kraus, Huang, and Keltner 2010). In this study, the researchers coded the physical touch behaviors of players during a season. They found that early-season touch predicted greater performance for individuals as well as teams later in the season. This was true even after they controlled for player status (something that affects touch behavior), preseason expectations, and early-season performance. Thus, touch, a very basic form of communication in teams, may be a factor that influences team cohesion.

Interestingly, when athletes feel that their team has high cohesion, they experience less cognitive anxiety and are more likely to see their cognitive and somatic symptoms of anxiety as helpful rather than overwhelming (Eys et al. 2003). This may be because the group members share the pressure—no one athlete is held responsible for wins or losses—and the athletes believe in the team's ability to manage the demands of competition. This undoubtedly comes with more practice, weathering hardships together, and knowing that the team can handle things as a group when facing adversity.

Thus, many factors contribute to cohesion on a team. Some of them are under your control, and some are not. To improve the cohesion on their teams, coaches can make adjustments to the factors that can be shaped. Creating experiences that help players get to know each other socially, build persistence in working on tasks, and increase adversity can help build a stronger, more bonded team.

Coaching Tips on Cohesion

Some activities that can help build cohesion are preseason team-building events. Early on, your goal is to help team members relax and get to know each other.

- A social gathering like a barbecue or picnic, or an outdoor activity like a hike or an adventure course, can be a good beginning. Icebreaker games that help players get to know each other help (e.g., two truths and a lie, where each player tells his or her partner two truths and a lie, and the partner or team has to guess which is the lie). Or ask the team to divide up based on two alternative likes and dislikes: for example, preferred season—winter or summer; sport they most love to watch—basketball or football; sport they most love to play; large party or smaller gathering of friends; reading or movies; pizza or fried chicken, and so on. Another fun icebreaker game is asking the question, "If you were a tool (or a kitchen gadget), which would you be (and why)?" All of these activities are meant to get players comfortable and getting to know each other.

- Some teams go away together for an overnight to a different location for training. This is not always possible due to logistics and money, but the idea of separating the team from their known surroundings can create an environment in which players have to get to know each other. In the famous film *Remember the Titans*, which is based on a true story, Coach Boon has a challenging task trying to build cohesion among a newly racially integrated football team. He takes them away from their hometown, forces a white and African American player to sit together on the bus and share rooms, puts them through extremely strenuous training, and motivates them with inspiring tales of the Civil War. His value and emphasis on uniting the team is clearly communicated. He also provides tough consequences for those who will not tolerate or abide by his rules. Obviously, he had quite the challenge, but forcing people to interact with each other, especially pairing those who are new to the team with more seasoned players, can help create connections.

- On a team, there are smaller subgroups and strong friendships. Ask players to match up with someone they don't know as well for drills, weight training, and such.

- Ask each member to share something about himself or herself. Make two circles with equal number of players in each. The inner circle faces the outer circle. Shift the circles by one player after the question has been answered until each person in the inner circle has talked to each person in the outer circle. Some prompts could be "Tell us about a great moment in your sporting life," "Who was your biggest support in your sports life?" or "Name three of your strengths and one thing you would like to improve in yourself as an athlete."

- When you do activities in pairs, ask players to match up with someone they don't know or they know less well. Athletes tend to pair with their closest buddies. This doesn't contribute to the overall cohesion of the group. By getting to know less-familiar players, athletes end up having more communication with the whole group, which can increase bonding to the group. This is essential early in the season when new players and transfers join the team.

- Create activities, games, or drills that involve physical touch on teams where cooperation is key. I believe touch is also good for teams that involve athletes who compete individually.

- Do a challenge course (like a ropes course) or a scavenger hunt together. Break the group into smaller groups and make it a competition.

Games to Build Cohesion

- Play games involving touch. One game that I have used involves about eight players in a circle and one player in the middle. For female athletes, have them cross their arms over their chests. For men, no need to cross the arms over the chest. They then hold their bodies stiff while tipping toward their teammates in the outside circle. Their feet remain anchored to one spot, so they literally bob from side to side, as their teammates support them, giving them a firm but gentle push to the other side of the circle. Make sure that the size of the athletes is somewhat matched for height and weight. This is literally a game of "I've got your back" as the player is pushed around in the circle.

- Separate the team into two lines of people, facing away from each other. They interlace their arms and sit back-to-back with their teammates (e.g., two lines of ten, sitting on the ground, back-to-back). They have to work together to stand up in unison and then sit down again. First time through, allow talking. Then ask players to do it again without talking, using only nonverbal signals. Another challenge is to do it with eyes closed.

- Divide the athletes into lines of eight to ten players. Have them line up sideways, binding their ankles to the player next to them in line with a rope or tie (for example, have the right ankle bound with a cloth tie to the left ankle of the player to the right of them in line, and the left ankle bound to the right ankle of the player to the left of them in line). Place three hoops or taped squares ahead of the line. The line has to move sideways together so that each member of the line steps both feet into each circle or square as the whole line proceeds through the hoops or squares. Sounds easy, but it's not! Takes a lot of coordination of movement.

- Have three thin ropes of approximately three feet in length. Make groups of four people. Each must hold a piece of the rope and not let go for any part of the activity. Ask the group to make a common slipknot in the center rope without any of the team letting go of the ropes. This is challenging, so allow for a little time. Notice who takes lead roles within the groups, or if a leader emerges. This can increase a group's willingness to use trial and error to solve problems.

- The human knot is a game where a group of individuals join arms across the circle with a buddy. They generally hold the hand of a different member of the circle with each hand. Then the group has to work together to unlock all arms. Do it once with talking, then without words for a challenge.

- Group teammates into small teams and then have them work together in tasks involving speed, rapid decision-making, balance, precise movements, gross motor movements—you design it based on your sport. It could involve shooting the ball, throwing the ball to a particular spot on the field, sprinting to another spot on the field, working together to accomplish some task that involves more than one teammate. If you time these races, it adds pressure.

In any sport, you can sequence important skills. For example, a batter is given three pitches to hit the ball to outfield; the outfielder has to catch it or field it, throw it to the basemen, who then has to throw it in to the catcher in a certain amount of time. Adding time pressure to a group task forces the group to work together more efficiently. Create an objective the group must meet—four successful hits in a certain amount of time.

- Life-size building tools can make for interesting games. Give players each a different role: talkers, runners, and builders. Give the talkers a design. Have the talkers describe it to the runners, who run to the builders and have to recommunicate and describe how to construct it. Then the builders actually make the structure. Ideally, the structure matches the original design.

Chapter 7

AROUSAL AND ANXIETY

You are watching one of your forwards in the middle of a soccer match, playing against a strong rival team. Your forward, Kayla, is doing great, playing her position well, passing, and also taking shots. You are excited by the energy and focus she has today. In the flash of a second, Kayla is fouled inside the box! Yes! It's a direct free penalty kick—what an opportunity! But then reality hits—you can see the stress on her face. She is clearly feeling the pressure. This player is so good! If you could just get her to relax and do what she knows how to do in practice. You watch as Kayla waits for the signal from the ref, and she moves toward the ball with power. It looks good, but you can tell the moment the ball leaves the ground it's too high. Such a lost opportunity!

As a coach, you often deal with situations in which individual athletes face pressure. You also watch whole teams crumble when the going gets tough. On every team, there are a variety of personalities, and how to coach them all well is a constant challenge. Some athletes thrive on the pressure, while others become easily overwhelmed and lose their focus. A number of the toughest-looking athletes get a case of nerves in competition. In addition, you attempt to energize them before games, but it doesn't always seem to help. These are some of the greatest questions in coaching. In this chapter, we'll examine the difference between arousal and anxiety and how both can influence the performance of your team.

Arousal

Arousal is an energizing function in the body, necessary to get the body moving and ready for vigorous activity (Sage 1984). There is a continuum of arousal, from highly activated (highly energized, heart pounding, high respiration) to sleep or coma states (low heart rate and reduced respiration). The heart rate is a primary control or measure of a person's arousal state (Selk 2009). Additionally, arousal can be experienced as both physical and psychological. But arousal is a neutral state. It is neither good nor bad, until the mind or perception makes it so. Only very high levels of arousal are interpreted by the mind as difficult; one's mind is convinced, when the heart rate is very high (the fight-or-flight heart rate is around 115–140 beats per minute), that survival is threatened and something is wrong—unless an athlete has been conditioned to respond differently. Some athletes like to be pumped up and work to increase their arousal before competing, while others try to reduce their level of arousal in order to be relaxed and focused during performance. A Russian sport psychologist by the name of Hanin identified something called the "individualized zone of optimal functioning," otherwise known as the IZOF or ZOF (Hanin 2000c). He used this concept to help explain differences in the need for certain levels of arousal for different sports; as an example, in weight lifting or sports using gross motor skills, higher levels of arousal are more helpful than in, say, golf putting or archery. When more precise fine motor movements are required, athletes do not perform well with too much arousal. Athletes need to be aware of their levels of arousal. For example, if athletes know they are too aroused, they can try to calm their bodies down before competing. Or, if they are sluggish, they can try to pump up their levels of arousal to be more ready for competition. The exercises at the end of this chapter will talk about different ways to help with this.

Anxiety

On the other hand, anxiety is an emotional and cognitive experience of recognizable, unpleasant feelings or thoughts that are disturbing. With anxiety, the negative experiences are characterized by changes in physical sensations and changes in mental experience. People don't like to feel anxious and think of it as uncomfortable. These feelings vary from mildly worried or uncomfortable to full-blown panic; they also change over time (Spielberger 1975). During an experience of anxiety, our autonomic nervous system (ANS) is activated; this is the system that controls our fight-or-flight response when we are stressed. Thus, when we are anxious, we are also aroused physically, although not all athletes who are aroused are anxious. Something additional is going on in the brain of the anxious athlete. Some signs of anxiety are as follows:

- cold, clammy hands
- constant need to urinate
- profuse sweating
- negative self-talk
- dazed look in the eyes
- feeling ill or nauseated
- headache
- dry mouth
- difficulty sleeping
- increased muscle tension
- butterflies in stomach
- inability to concentrate
- consistently better performance in practice than in competition (Weinberg and Gould 2011)

Some athletes are temperamentally more anxious. They may have had stressful childhoods, or their nervous systems are more reactive, possibly from birth. Most parents know these differences exist in their very young children. Some kids fall down and make a big fuss, and others pop right up and act like nothing happened. There are calm babies and fussy babies. However, we know that all children and adults occasionally experience anxiety.

People who have studied anxiety differentiate between *state anxiety* (anxiety that is based on the situation) versus *trait anxiety* (a person who has a tendency to get anxious across lots of situations) (Spielberger 1975). This is especially relevant to sport, where competitive situations tend to cause anxiety. Those who have trait anxiety—who tend toward anxiety on a regular basis—have more difficulty in challenging situations that are uncertain and important. Athletes who have state anxiety, however, feel anxiety mainly in critical moments of play during competition. Some athletes struggle with both; they may struggle with anxiety on a day-to-day basis in their lives, and then they may experience an additional dose of anxiety in competition. For example, in a basketball game, a critical moment might be when there are ten seconds left in the game, and the score is tied, and a player is fouled and called to the free-throw line. The pressure is on, as he or she knows that this point may decide the game. Or, in baseball, the bases are loaded, a batter is up, and there are two outs. Whether an athlete feels in control as the pressure increases seems to be a critical factor in determining whether his or her reactions to these high-stakes situations cause a choke versus a clutch performance. Maintaining external focus is key because when people become more anxious, their attention is often turned inward to internal thoughts (too much thinking), visual changes (tunnel vision under extreme anxiety with the loss of peripheral vision), increased heart rate, muscle tension, labored respiration, and so on. A highly anxious athlete is no longer focused on what's going on around him or her. The following changes may occur in attention, concentration, and visual search when we are anxious:

- narrowing of attention
- shift to dominant style (if an athlete tends toward narrow attention versus broad, he or she will go to their preferred style)

- changes in gaze and eye fixations
- an increase in performance worries, situation-irrelevant thoughts, and thoughts of escape
- possible changes in working memory
- attending to inappropriate cues (Weinberg and Gould 2011)

Dealing with Anxiety in Athletes

While choking is a loss of performance under high-pressure conditions, athletes who tend toward anxiety may constantly feel that their performance suffers. In order to help these individuals manage anxiety, it is important to note that anxiety can be experienced as somatic (bodily) or in the mind (cognitive). Some people have a lot of physical reactivity to stress (e.g., increased heart rate, muscle tension, etc.), and others have lots of negative thoughts that get in their way. The methods for dealing with anxiety try to focus on one or the other of these problems. Relaxation methods try to reduce muscle tension, slow the breath, and reduce heart rate (more physical). Mindfulness practice works on acceptance of emotions and thoughts without judgment, and refocusing the attention on the breath in the here and now. Over time, this can improve a person's ability to allow problematic thoughts and feelings to pass, and increases a person's ability to focus his or her attention. So there are muscle-to-mind and mind-to-muscle methods for reducing the experience of anxiety. We will outline some of those methods shortly.

One method of working on reducing anxiety is to intervene on a thought level by teaching people not to interpret high-arousal states as problematic. When the heart rate goes up and we are breathing heavily, the mental response or interpretation can be one of two things: *this is a problem*, or *my body is highly activated*. Putting athletes into these situations by stressing them (high-pressure training situations) helps athletes experience this. Competition often has the impact of increasing these arousal levels even more because of the outcome pressure. But coaches can try to influence how athletes interpret high-pressure situations. By *reframing* (a word we use in psychology that means *changing the meaning*) the highly competitive situation as exciting, energizing, and what we train for, coaches can help athletes learn to love high-stakes situations. Obviously, physical preparation is absolutely critical, because preparation helps produce confidence. But how a team or individual athletes think about this, and your communicated belief in their ability to handle it, also affects their ability to learn to cope with competition.

You are probably wondering how a coach can teach athletes not to interpret things negatively on the court or field. When you are in the middle of scrimmaging and your players are physically stretching their limits (they are sweating, exhausted, looking at you like you are killing them), call a time-out and tell them this is what they need to learn to love—they are pushing their limits, working their bodies to the max, and this is what is good and will help them to perform well under pressure and win games. This is a positive "reframe" of their high physical exertion.

In other situations, during a tough game or match, during the time-outs or halftime speech, you can tell them that this is truly exciting and good—that they are learning to love the competition, that you believe in them, and that they have the capacity to fight intensely. Belief is one of the most important things you can offer to anxious athletes, because often their thoughts include self-doubts. Verbal persuasion is key among the factors in building confidence or self-efficacy (the belief in one's ability to successfully do something) (Bandura 1997). Behind every successful athlete is a parent or a coach who helped him or her to believe in himself or herself. As a coach, you continue this process, helping to transform their experiences. When athletes are afraid or anxious, you can put it in a positive light, you can nurture their love of high-stakes situations, and you can say, "It's okay to fear this, but you can accept it and move beyond fear."

A number of methods can be taught to athletes to help them manage anxiety. Some of these techniques come from clinical psychology, and others have already been adapted and taught to athletes. They are as follows:

Relaxation Training

This ranges from progressive muscle relaxation (PMR), which is a form of going through various muscle groups and tensing and then relaxing the muscles, to autogenics, a method in which verbal statements guide the person into a state of relaxation. In the following section, I will provide several examples or techniques of relaxation training, as well as scripts. You can introduce these exercises in practice, but athletes need to be encouraged to work with these methods outside of practice on their own.

Progressive Muscle Relaxation

Progressive muscle relaxation (PMR) involves the tensing and then relaxing of each muscle group of the body, one group at a time. This method involves minimal movement to relax the muscles, which appeals to athletes who are tired. It can also lower blood pressure, heart rate, and respiration. Using this exercise, you can teach your players the difference between highly tense muscles and relaxed muscles. As they get better at this, they can isolate groups of muscles that they want to relax, while allowing for more tension in certain muscle groups. Relaxed muscles fire faster and are less prone to injury. You can demonstrate this by having athletes tense their fingers in one hand and then ask them to alternately tap the index and the middle finger while still holding the tension in the fingers (Hanton, Mellalieu, and Williams 2015). Then ask them to relax the fingers and ask them to repeat this. This exercise is an easy way to demonstrate how much better relaxed muscles work.

Some people prefer to listen to an audio recording that guides them through progressive muscle relaxation. The scripts are usually about twenty minutes long, but an abbreviated version can be done with less time, particularly as a person gets more experienced with the technique. There are a number of them available on the Internet. See https://www.anxietybc.com/sites/default/files/MuscleRelaxation.pdf for some helpful instructions. Progressive muscle relaxation may be done sitting or lying down. For an added benefit, have the athlete inhale when tensing the muscles and exhale when releasing the contraction.

Instructions

(This exercise has been adapted from the progressive muscle relaxation exercise in *Comprehensive Stress Management* by Jerrold Greenberg, 2011.)

Have the coach, captain, or trainer lead the exercise with the following script (you may adapt it for your sport):

> We are going to do an exercise called progressive muscle relaxation. In this exercise, you will learn to notice the difference between tense and relaxed muscles. You will also get the benefit of relaxing tense muscles, which promotes a feeling of warmth and relaxation in the body.
>
> We will start with the right arm. First, tense the right fist. Hold the tension; notice the tension and the tightness in the fingers, forearm, and hand. Breathe in and hold the breath for several seconds as you tense the muscles. (Pause.) Now release the tension, allowing the fingers to relax completely. Repeat this one more time with the right fist.
>
> (Pause between muscle groups for a few seconds.)
>
> Now breathe in deeply and hold the breath as you tense the left fist. Notice the tension. Hold it. (Pause.) Now release. Allow the fingers to uncurl and relax, completely relaxing the arm.

Next, bend your arms at the elbows and tighten up the biceps like you are trying to show off your muscles. Inhale as you tense, hold the breath, and slowly exhale as you release the tension. Let the arms drop to your side and allow them to completely relax. (Pause.) Repeat this once more.

Next, tighten the muscles of your eyes and forehead, scrunching them closed. Hold the tension and then release, picturing a smooth forehead. (Pause.) Next, make an exaggerated frown, tightening the muscles around the mouth and jaw. Hold the tension for several seconds. Now release, smoothing and relaxing the facial muscles, deepening the relaxation.

Next, tighten the jaws by clenching your teeth together. Hold the tension; notice it and then release it. Relax the jaws. Breathe slowly. Now purse the lips by pressing your lips together tightly. Hold the tension and then release. Imagine the stillness and relaxation spreading all across your face.

Next, lean your head back as far as you can. Feel the tension in the neck. Then roll your head to the right, feeling the tension. Then roll your head to the left. Last, bring your head to center and press your chin to your chest. Now bring your head up to a neutral position, facing in front of you.

Next shrug the shoulders. Hold them tense and notice the tension. After a brief time, release the shoulders. Repeat. Make sure to roll the shoulders back.

Next, move down to the abdomen. Harden the abdominal muscles as though you are trying to make your belly firm. Hold the tension; notice it and then release. Repeat.

Next, tighten the thighs and the buttocks. Hold the tension. When you release the tension, release the breath. You can also anchor the feet on the ground while tensing this muscle group, pressing the feet hard into the ground. Repeat.

For the lower legs and feet, tighten the calves and shins by pointing the toes upward. Hold the tension and then release. For the feet, point the toes and curl them under. Then release the tension.

You may repeat relaxing and tensing muscle groups that you have already done to relax them further. By now, your body is warm and relaxed. When you are ready to come back to the moment, tune into the sounds around you. I am going to count backwards from three to one. When I reach one, open your eyes, noticing how calm and relaxed you feel.

Deep Diaphragmatic Breathing

I like Jason Selk's coverage of the centering breath in his book *10-Minute Toughness* (2009). He suggests a fifteen-second process whereby an athlete breathes in for six seconds, holds the breath for two seconds, and exhales for seven seconds or (6–2–7). According to Selk, athletes younger than twelve years of age should inhale for four seconds, hold for two seconds, exhale for five seconds (4–2–5). Yogic breathing is also described as 1:2 ratio of inhalation count to exhalation count. So if you inhale for four seconds, you exhale for eight seconds. Both of these methods have the impact of lowering the heart rate and decreasing one's arousal level. *Box breathing* (also called four-square breathing or square-box breathing) is another method that can be used when an athlete is fearful, angry, or frustrated (highly emotionally aroused). When using this method, an athlete inhales for four seconds, holds the breath for four seconds, exhales for four seconds, and holds the breath again for four seconds. This method can help with releasing tension and frustration as well, so that an athlete can shift his or her attention back to the task at hand.

One thing to mention is that when practicing these methods of breathing, you should consider that a count of one is really spoken or thought as "one, one thousand." Also, the breath should be from the abdomen, low in the belly. If an individual is having a hard time breathing deeply and getting the lower abdomen to fill with air, have him or her place and keep the tongue on the roof of the mouth while inhaling and exhaling. When people are highly anxious, they breathe shallowly and up high in the chest. This can cause hyperventilation, which may cause a number of physical symptoms: dizziness; tingling in the lips, hands, or feet; headache; weakness; or fainting.

Autogenics Training

This is a method that was developed by a German physician named Dr. Schulz in 1932, for the purposes of health promotion and relaxation. He devised this method to be self-directed and hoped it would help with insomnia, blood pressure, and so on. Schulz drew from hypnosis and yoga to create this approach. The beauty of autogenics is that you don't actually have to do anything to the muscles but simply go through a series of verbal statements (spoken out loud by the leader of the exercise). It is a nice one to do when athletes are particularly tired (like the body scan, mentioned in the mindfulness meditation section). I have also advised clients to record their own voice directing the exercise on their cell phone, and then listen to it when they do the exercise outside of team practice. The following are sample statements:

> My right arm is heavy. (Repeat four times.)
> My right arm is warm. (Repeat four times.)
> My right arm is tingly. (Repeat two times.)
> My right arm is heavy and warm and tingly.
> (Repeat four times.)
> (Follow with left arm, right leg, left leg.)

> This method moves through the areas of the body, focusing on sensations of heaviness and warmth in the muscles. Most

people become proficient in a matter of a few weeks by practicing two or three times daily for five to ten minutes. Some athletes I have worked with like this method because they can use it before they sleep. The sensation of warmth and heaviness in the limbs is often experienced when one is deeply relaxed.

Another version of autogenic training consists of seven formulas that you repeat in a specific pattern:

> I am completely calm (once).
> My right arm is heavy (six times).
> I am completely calm (once).
> My right arm is warm (six times).
> I am completely calm (once).
> My heart beats calmly and regularly (six times).
> I am completely calm (once).
> My breathing is calm and regular ... it breathes me (six times).
> I am completely calm (once).
> My abdomen is flowingly warm (six times).
> I am completely calm (once).
> My forehead is pleasantly cool (six times).
> I am completely calm (once).
> Source: http://www.welz.us/Autogenic.pdf

Mindfulness Meditation

Most mindfulness approaches that help alleviate anxiety are based on mindfulness-based stress reduction (MBSR), an approach credited to Jon Kabat-Zinn (1991), who developed this intervention as a way to help people who were suffering from acute or chronic illnesses to manage stress. Since that time, MBSR has been applied to many groups—including athletes, to help with performance—by increasing present-moment focus and attention as well as relaxation. It is an approach that takes a position of compassion and nonjudgment toward the self. This is quite contrary to the hard-nosed approach of many tough, authoritarian-style coaches. However, there is much promise to this approach as applied to sports. What I believe is most helpful about this approach is that it flies in the face of perfectionism, which often adds to stress in high-level athletes and may increase performance pressure.

I have used a workbook called *Mindfulness-Based Stress Reduction: A Workbook*, by Elisha Goldstein and Jonathan Stahl (2010). It contains a number of meditation scripts and is based on Jon Kabat-Zinn's approach. One of my favorite exercises is the "5-Minute Mindful Breathing Meditation." The gist of this exercise is slowing down the thoughts, focusing in on the breath, and allowing any thoughts to pass away without being judgmental of ourselves. The focus on the breath is wherever the person feels it—the nose, neck, chest, or belly (or somewhere else). Phrases like "There's no place to go and nothing else to do. Just be here in the moment, noticing the breath, living life one inhalation and one exhalation at a time" (Goldstein and Stahl 2010) help the individual to slow down and simply focus on the moment, the breath, and let everything else pass.

Another is the body scan, which athletes often love because they can move through the various areas of the body and scan for tension. They don't do anything but notice it and continue to breathe, perhaps sending the breath to that area. Often a person can become aware of tension he or she is holding in the body without awareness. There are longer versions (fifteen-minute and thirty-minute) in the book as well, and it comes with a CD they can load onto their phones. Practiced frequently, these exercises can be used precompetition, before or after practice, at home, or during halftime to quiet the body and focus the attention.

In previous chapters, I discussed the research on mindfulness and its impact on our brain. But we must practice this, just as physical skills are practiced, in order for it to have lasting impacts. Mindfulness meditation, while it can be effective momentarily, is of most benefit when practiced on a regular basis. Most people who enjoy it adopt a daily practice, even if brief. In clinical practice, a number of individuals who have anxiety problems have been able to get off of medication by engaging in regular mindfulness practice. George Mumford's recently released book called *The Mindful Athlete* (2015) is a good read for anyone wishing to learn more about how mindfulness can be used in sports. Mumford worked with Phil Jackson when he coached the Lakers, and he also worked with Jackson when he was employed by the Knicks.

In addition, there are a couple of books that have developed specific approaches for athletes that incorporate mindfulness training. The two exercises following this paragraph are shortened versions, adapted from Gardner and Moore's (2007) book, and integrated with the mindfulness-based stress reduction exercises (like the five minutes mindful breathing discussed above). These are basic versions of the mindfulness of the breath, which is one of the core exercises of MBSR. I have used this approach with athletes and have found it to be helpful. It is a little different from the pure MBSR approach. It has athletes look at their values, their goals, and what behaviors and thoughts get in the way. It draws from the acceptance and commitment therapy (ACT) approach, which is an offshoot of cognitive behavioral therapy (Hayes, Strosahl, and Wilson 1999).

Exercise 1: Mindfulness of the Breath (adapted from Gardner and Moore 2007 and Goldstein and Stahl 2010)

> This exercise will help you to develop your mindfulness and attention skills and help you learn to be in the present moment. Find a comfortable sitting position. (Pause.) Notice the places your body touches the chair and the contact your feet make with the ground. Allow your eyes to close if you are comfortable. Otherwise, look down and soften your gaze. (Pause.) Take several deep breaths. Notice the air going in and out of your body, wherever you observe it the most. For some people, it is at the tip of the nose; for others, the belly, the chest, or somewhere else. (Pause.) Wherever your focus is, notice your breath coming in and

out of your body. (Pause.) You do not need to control your breath or count the breaths. Simply allow the breath to come and go, one inhalation and one exhalation at a time. (Pause.) At times, you may find that your attention wanders from the breath. Notice where you traveled in your mind, and then, without becoming critical of yourself, simply draw the attention back to the breath. It is normal to have many different thoughts and emotions that come and go from your mind. (Pause.) Just allow these thoughts or feelings to float by and then refocus your attention on the breath. Right at this moment, there is no place to go and nothing else to do. Just be in the here and now, observing the breath. (Pause.) When you are ready, slowly open your eyes, move your hands and feet, look around at your physical surroundings, and go on with the rest of your day.

Exercise 2: Centering Breath (shortened and adapted from Gardner and Moore 2007)

Find a comfortable sitting position. Allow your eyes to close gently. (Pause.) Breathe in and out slowly and deeply several times. Notice the sound and the feel of your own breath as you inhale and exhale. (Pause.)

Now, focus your attention on your surroundings. What sounds are occurring inside the room? What sounds do you notice outside the room? (Pause.) Shift your attention to the places where your body has contact with the chair you are sitting in. Notice any sensations that are present in the rest of your body. (Pause.) Don't try to change these sensations. Just observe them.

Next, notice any thoughts you may be having about this exercise. Just notice any thoughts, reservations, or worries, as though you are watching them pass by without any attachment to them. (Pause.) Don't try to make them go away; just watch them and notice. (Pause.) Next, consider what you would like to be able do in your athletic life today. How would you like your skills to develop? Where would you like your focus to be? What is important to you? (Pause.)

Sit for another few moments and slowly bring your focus to the room. Listen to any sounds you are hearing inside or outside the room. Again, notice your breathing. Slowly open your eyes and connect with the room around you. Notice how your mind and body feel.

Both of the above exercises help increase an athlete's attention to his or her breath, to the here and now, and attempts to slow down extraneous thought. I have used both of these exercises with athletes and my sport psychology students. At first, they are not so sure about them. However, as I do them repeatedly, they tell me they grow more comfortable and find them helpful. Keep in mind that some of the athletes will have been exposed to something like this if they have done yoga classes. However, some young people have not encountered exercises like this and will find them foreign at first.

Keith Kaufmann and his colleagues at Catholic University have developed a program called Mindfulness for Sport Performance Enhancement. They also have a series of mindfulness exercises. Kaufmann and his colleagues modeled their approach on Jon Kabat-Zinn's MBSR model. The exercises in their approach are somewhat longer than those in the MAC approach developed by Gardner and Moore (2007). My experience working with athletes is that some of them have a hard time with the lengthier mindfulness exercises.

To summarize, in this chapter I have tried to distinguish between arousal and anxiety. Additionally, I hope you have some new ideas about how to help athletes and teams deal with anxiety and become more effective at managing this challenging emotion. The more you can increase awareness of these emotions and teach strategies to deal with them, the greater the sense of control that athletes will have when they encounter these challenges in games and competition.

Coaching Tips for Arousal and Anxiety

- Athletes should learn to recognize high levels of arousal in their bodies and their optimal levels of arousal for performance of their sport. Teach athletes to become aware of their heart rates as the primary source of information regarding their arousal levels.

- Athletes benefit from learning about anxiety and recognizing symptoms of anxiety in their bodies to help prevent performance slips.

- Help athletes to learn not to view high-arousal states as problematic. Reframe these states as the athlete being prepared, ready, and optimal.

- Teach methods of relaxation and arousal management, such as progressive muscle relaxation, autogenics training, diaphragmatic breathing, and mindfulness meditation. Help athletes to think of mental training as just as vital as physical training, especially for those with a tendency toward anxious dispositions.

- Practice these techniques with your team.

Chapter 8

CHOKING

Your team has done really well in today's competition, but the other team has rallied in this last five minutes of the game. The score is tied. You are watching, trying to call out reassuring messages to your team. "Play your game!" They begin to look like they are moving too fast, and a turnaround occurs in the other team's favor. You call a time-out. "Settle down, guys! Let's just execute." You direct them to a particular play, with an emphasis on getting fouled offensively. You watch as they go back out there with more poise and begin to do what you know they know how to do. However, the other team gets lucky and shoots a field goal successfully. Your team gets the rebound and charges down the court for a layup. The other team is now one point ahead. Your player gets fouled, and you are delighted. He is one of the best free-throw shooters on your team, with an average around 82 percent. He steps up to the line, and you can tell he is nervous. Every point matters. He doesn't seem to be doing his normal preshot routine. You want to scream, "Trust yourself! Do it like you do all the time!" You watch as he misses the first shot and makes the second. You are now into overtime play. Had he just made both shots! You would be heading back to the locker room to congratulate them on a critical win.

Sian Beilock, a psychologist from the University of Chicago who studies human performance, is the author of the book *Choke: What the Secrets of the Brain Reveal About Getting It Right When You Have To* (2010). She has studied choking behavior in sports, in academia, and in business. And she has some ideas on how to prevent choking. But first, let's look at how she defines choking:

"Choking is suboptimal performance, not just poor performance. It's a performance that is inferior to what you can do and have done in the past. We all have performance ups and downs, but choking occurs when performers perceive a situation to be highly stressful and, because of the stress, they screw up. Choking is most noticeable when an opportunity to win is squandered, perhaps because this is when the pressure to excel is at its highest. Choking is not random" (Beilock 2010).

How do we break cycles of choking? Beilock suggests that a psychological concept called *desensitization* may contain the answer. Systematic desensitization is a clinical technique to help people who have phobias or high levels of fear of particular things (Wolpe 1969). Take the situation of a fear of elevators. By exposing someone to the feared situation or object gradually (in a sequence of steps where the first step is to imagine the elevator and the last step is to ride the elevator) and teaching them to relax at the same time, they gradually learn to manage their fear of elevators. Thus, if we expose athletes to stressful conditions, they should habituate or get used to it over time (Beilock 2010). In terms of practice, this means that we increase stressors to mimic the competitive environment. Lots of coaches do this already by practicing in gyms with crowd noise, buzzers on, and similar conditions. In addition, coaches can interrupt athletes during practice and place them in high-pressure situations. An example would be bringing basketball players to the free-throw line unexpectedly.

Southern Utah University's coach, Roger Reid, did just this. During the middle of a practice scrimmage, when the players were least expecting it, Coach Reid would stop everything and send his players to the free-throw line. If the player made his shot, he got to rest and catch his breath. If he missed, he would have to sprint around the court. This is a form of punishment that is used effectively to increase the stakes and add pressure to performance. When Reid started at Southern Utah, the team was horrible at free-throw shots, ranking 217th. Two years later, at the time the *New York Times* featured an article about free throws and the lack of improvement over the past forty years of basketball, Reid's team ranked number one and had an average of just over 80 percent (Branch 2009). By increasing the pressured practice situations, he helped his players habituate or desensitize to high stress. As a result, competitive play was not such a radical shift from practice.

Jason Selk, in his book *10-Minute Toughness*, tells a story about former Major League Baseball pitcher Mike Mussina. When he was a kid, Mike's dad put a strike zone on their barn and built his son a mound sixty feet away. While pitching to the strike zone on the barn, Mike pictured himself pitching in the Major Leagues. He would think about himself pitching well in high-pressure situations. When Mussina moved from Baltimore to play for the Yankees, the press asked him how he was going to handle the stress of pitching under the watchful eye of the New York baseball scene. He calmly answered that, when he was a kid, he often imagined himself pitching well in the high-stakes games. Now as an adult, when the pressure was high, he would imagine himself throwing to the strike zone on the barn. In this way, he upped the ante, increasing the arousal level when he practiced, and then in the actual games, he reduced his arousal by pretending he was back at the barn (Selk 2009). This is a great example of using imagery and the mind to intensify stress while training and reducing the intensity of stress when competing.

Temperamentally anxious (trait anxious) athletes may actually need more practice in stressful circumstances to get accustomed to stress. Giving them ample opportunities to practice under pressure helps them to adapt to and manage in highly stressful circumstances. They may also need to be taught methods to reduce the reactivity of their bodies and minds. That is where practices like mindfulness meditation and deep diaphragmatic breath training come in. These exercises can be taught in practice and benefit all athletes;

they can then be practiced more often outside of structured practice times for those who may need to work more deeply on this issue. See the exercises at the end of this chapter for scripts on how to do this with your teams.

Additional tools that may help to prevent choking are teaching athletes to focus on certain things and not others. Beilock discusses paralysis by analysis, or a process of paying too much attention to activities (or motor skills) that are normally outside of one's conscious attention. She studied highly skilled college soccer players and asked them to dribble a soccer ball through a series of cones while paying attention to the side of their foot that was making contact with the ball (Beilock et al. 2002). They did this in an effort to get the players to pay attention to something that might not normally be in their conscious focus. They found that players dribbled more slowly and made more mistakes when they paid attention to their foot compared to when they dribbled without any instructions to pay attention. The implications of this research are that being overly tuned in to the actual movements (that the athlete knows very well) will bring about more errors in movement. Beilock suggests that focusing on a strategy (what to do) rather than technique (how to do it) can help prevent choking under stressful conditions. An example of this was a study on soccer players by Robin Jackson and his colleagues. He asked one group to focus on technique while dribbling (e.g., keep loose with knees bent), and another group focused on outcome (e.g., keep the ball close to the cones). The strategy group (focused on outcome, or *what* to do) performed better than the technique group (focused on their knees, or *how* to do it) (Jackson, Ashford, and Norsworthy 2006).

A similar study was conducted with Division I baseball players. They were asked to take batting practice in a hitting simulator and at the same time pay attention to whether their bat was moving downward or upward during the hitting movement (Gray 2004). As a result, their performance suffered. This suggests that we need to keep the mind clear of overanalyzing something that is automatic and doesn't require conscious attention.

Research on the neuroscience of expert athletes in sports that demand high concentration, such as marksmen, suggests that the expert's brain, when monitored via electrodes, looks calmer than the novice's brain. Hatfield found that skilled rifle shooters showed less neural activity during the aiming period just before they were about to pull the trigger. Anxious athletes often describe the flood of negative self-talk or chatter that occupies their mind preperformance. Thus, for anxious athletes or those who have a hard time quieting their minds, humming a well-known tune or paying attention to a sensory detail like the feel of their hands on the bat as they step into the batter's box can keep the left frontal lobe's activity low. This might offer anxious athletes a focus that allows their muscle memory to take over without the mind interfering. This suggestion came from an experience in the classroom when I asked a baseball pitcher (who was on the Division I team at the university) to participate in a focus exercise. The exercise involved throwing at a target, trying to hit the bull's-eye. He was able to do it reaching a very high rate of hitting the target under the baseline condition. Under the distraction condition, in which someone was trying to disrupt his concentration, he matched his baseline. Asked what he was doing, he said he was humming a familiar tune in his head to help his concentration.

Additionally, Beilock discusses the work of a psychologist for the Canadian swim team, Hap Davis, who came up with an innovative way to reduce the effect of their athletes' failures, something that could help an athlete regroup after a bad mistake (Beilock 2010). Davis developed a method that helps swimmers look at their failures from a more positive perspective. He and a team of neuroscientists looked at the brain activity (using fMRI) of swimmers watching a video of a fairly recent failed performance. What he found was increased activity in the emotional centers of the brain and reduced activity in the motor regions of the brain connected with planning and execution of movement. If the swimmers engaged in his three-step intervention—(1) expressed the feelings they had when they watched the failed race; (2) thought about what went wrong in the actual swim (e.g., my kick was too slow); and (3) imagined performance changes for the next race—then they had less emotion-related brain activity and more activity in important motor regions of the brain (Davis et al. 2008). The implication is that if an athlete blows an early race during a competition, it may help him or her to put this into practice and create a strategic plan for the subsequent races. According to Beilock (2010), Davis has actually put this into action with swimmers poolside after a bad performance. This helps the athlete to shift out of a negative mind-set after a failure.

Pausing in order to interrupt a negative mind-set or anxious state during competition may also help. A batter who recognizes that negative thinking is running through his or her mind may step out of the batting box and refocus.

A deep, clearing breath, an affirming thought (see the ball, hit the ball, smooth and relaxed), and then refocusing on whatever their personal routine is as they step back up to the plate. Seeing a successful hit in one's mind before stepping into the box can also set up positive expectancy and not trigger the fear response. Jason Selk, a sport psychologist who works a lot with baseball players, suggests that players practice viewing the personal highlight reel (running an imaginary video of a successful execution of a skill) as a way of setting up the athlete for success. He also emphasizes what he calls a centering breath (Selk 2009). Often, you can watch excellent free-throw shooters go through the clearing breath, the exact preshot routine, and then *boom*, you watch them score the basket.

> The beauty of this relationship between attention and anxiety is that it gives us a tool to manage anxiety. If you find yourself becoming anxious, all you have to do is let your attention drift back to the here and now and your anxiety will dissipate. (Lardon 2008)

Coaching Tips for Preventing Choking

Practice under pressured conditions:

- Expose athletes to repeated high-pressure conditions to help them desensitize to stressful conditions.
- Surprise athletes by interrupting them and putting them under pressure to perform (e.g.,

with free throws, penalty shots, batting). Also, add consequences to their performance as a way to increase pressure.

- Teach athletes about the power of deep breathing and mindfulness-type practices as tools to manage their arousal levels and reduce arousal in high-pressure situations. Emphasize the need to repeatedly practice this off the court or field, in order to be able to use it in competition.

- Help athletes to use their imaginations while practicing to see themselves in stressful competitive situations. You can also create the conditions (e.g., game is tied, two outs, bases loaded, and you are up; fifteen seconds left in basketball game that is tied, and you are at the foul line; for football field-goal kickers, last few seconds of tied game, and you're up for a field goal kick).

- Add time pressure by hurrying your athletes in order to add pressure.

- When athletes choke during a game or competition, pull them aside and ask them how they feel, what they did, and how they can change this in the next play, race, or match. This processing moves the activity out of the emotional centers of the brain and helps an athlete shift to a more positive mind-set.

- Teach athletes to follow preperformance routines that help them get out of their heads and focus on the relevant things in the environment.

Chapter 9

SLUMPS

One of your players who is typically at the top of the batting order has been having a terrible season. Last year, her batting average was amazing, but this year she has hit a wall. She is still an incredible fielder, and as her coach, you don't want to pull her from play. But she is not performing. You have talked to her, and there doesn't seem to be anything upsetting going on in her life. She is a senior, and sometimes there is a lot of pressure if the athlete doesn't know what she wants to do after graduation. But she has been so consistent over her college career. It really makes you feel awful for her. You've encouraged her to persist, to keep doing the drills in practice, and to try to do some extra hitting practice on her own. But what else can you do as her coach?

What is a slump? It's a period of less-than-optimal performance during which an athlete often gets discouraged. It differs from choking in that choking is a onetime event, whereas a slump can go on for some time. This could be a period of poor shooting in basketball, an inability to score or defend in soccer, or a series of strikeouts in baseball or softball. Maybe it is a failure to achieve a certain time or improve times in running or swimming. Or it could be a series of losses, such as in tennis or in wrestling. Slumps may follow a period of success or optimal performance, and as a result, a slump can be perceived as devastating by the athlete. Sometimes there are physical reasons behind a slump (e.g., recovery from an injury). Other times, it is a mental reason that is causing an athlete to lose his or her competitive edge. There could be personal stressors, such as relationship problems, academic struggles, financial issues, or family concerns. This chapter will consider the impact of slumps on athletes, as well as how to coach athletes through a slump.

The Origins of Slumps

Athletes can go through periods of intense personal doubt about their abilities, engaging in self-analysis, questioning what is going on, and trying to make adjustments to get back to their sweet spot. They may ask why they are playing, believe they are not good enough, or fear that they may never again achieve the level of play that they once enjoyed. Athletes transitioning to college-level play with increased expectations can often do a number on their heads. Many college players have had the constant support of their parents, and they are operating in an environment that is less connected to that support for the first time. I have been surprised by how many college athletes have been coached by their parents. If they weren't coached by their parents, they have often had the consistent support of their parents, who frequently attended their games or competitions. This intense involvement can be quite different from the relationship with a college coach, who may be more detached.

Regardless of the reasons for the slump, coaches play an important role in helping an athlete to recover his or her level of play. One method of helping athletes is trying to get them to shift to a positive perspective. Rather than focusing on what they cannot achieve, help an athlete know that slumps are a normal part of athletic life. Working through dips in performance takes persistence and fortitude. Refining skills is something that can be done with effort. This does not mean you want the athlete in his or her head, thinking; an athlete who is overanalyzing does not trust that the slump will pass. By continuing to work hard and learning to relax in practice and in competition, an athlete can achieve a quiet patience in terms of his or her attitude toward the slump. Essentially, poor performance increases pressure to right the wrong of a previous performance, increasing an athlete's typical level of arousal. This increasing arousal, or stress and fear, can throw off coordination.

You often see this after an individual makes a mistake in a competition. That athlete will often go to drastic measures to show the coach he or she can make it up. This has resulted in desperate overdrive kinds of efforts that frequently do not work. Instead, relaxing and letting go of the previous failure, then reminding oneself to focus on the next play is a better strategy. Staying out of one's head is critical. Depending on what type of sport is being engaged in, this can eat up vital seconds and shift attention away from the present moment. Using a cue phrase to reinstruct oneself as to where to focus attention can remind the athlete not to go inward. Even the simple phrase of "see the play" or "next opportunity" can tell the athletes where to place their eyes, which is often where their attention will be.

The idea of "next play" was discussed at length by Jay Bilas in his book, *Toughness: Developing True Strength On and Off the Court* (2013). He elaborates on the importance of basketball players quickly shifting their attention from the last play to the next play. He also talks about players taking too long to celebrate a success and how this can result in missing the next play. When I have observed practice in basketball, emotionally invested players who miss a shot will sometimes slam the post or the walls of the gym to emphasize their disappointment. I often wonder if this is done to express frustration or to let the coach know how invested they are. But this is wasted energy. They need to let it go and not expend any more time or energy on a moment that is now in the past. It does not mean they don't care; it just means they are focused on the next chance to score or make the play. One lost shot should not dictate how they respond. The ability to let it roll off their shoulders should be practiced. A short memory for failures is a positive feature in a player. Perfectionist athletes often have problems with this because they are so focused on not having made the last play.

> I've missed more than 9,000 shots in my career. I've lost almost 300 games. 26 times, I've been trusted to take the game-winning shot and missed. I've failed over and over and over again in my life. And that is why I succeed.
>
> —Michael Jordan

An athlete who is struggling over a long period of time might benefit from trying to focus on his or her individual strengths as a player. This can keep their emphasis on the positive. Coaches can also be helpful to them by continuously offering support and belief that they will get back into their rhythm. Obviously, athletes are different in how much verbal support they might want from the coach. Going silent on players may increase their perception of your disapproval or detachment and may create fear. Instead, help them focus their practice, talk to them about what they are experiencing, and help them to keep the faith that this is a temporary phenomenon.

> Hall of Famer Frank Robinson had one of the greatest rookie seasons in baseball history, but in his second season, he had an 0-for-20 slump, and 35 years later acknowledged, "I didn't think I was ever going to get another hit." (Kurkjian 2012)

Doing an analysis of whether it is a physical, emotional, or mental problem is important. Additionally, setting goals for practice, outside practice and competition, can help to focus efforts on mastery. If there are issues outside of athletics, such as academic struggles or personal problems, a player needs to consider getting some help with these. But the message related to performance of skills needs to be to trust the process and allow the player to relax. Nothing can hurt a player more than increased pressure and being hyper-focused on performance. When we are in flow or the zone, we are not thinking about what we are doing; we are not considering our performance under a magnifying glass. In fact, we are often not thinking at all. We are *playing,* often enjoying the moment completely. The idea of totally accepting ourselves and where we are, performance-wise, is important. Compassion toward self—without losing the discipline and focus of practice—is one of the key building blocks to getting out of a slump.

Counteracting Slumps

One exercise that may help an athlete move into an appreciative frame of mind and less-dissatisfied perspective is keeping a gratitude journal. Ask the athlete to write down three to five things every few days that he or she is thankful for. This promotes a continual focus on what's right in their athletic life. Recognizing and recording things such as, "I am not injured, I can still catch and field well even if my batting has been off, I have great teammates, and I am strong," can keep athletes thinking in a positive direction. Labeling what's right keeps it in our focus and tends to help people feel better. Emmons and McCullough (2003) found that people who practiced gratitude were in better physical health, exercised more, and had greater levels of well-being.

In another study, those who had a more grateful attitude had lower levels of stress hormones in their blood (McCraty et al. 1998). So this simple act of adjusting our attitude on a regular basis can shift our minds into a less-stressed mode of operation.

Another suggestion is having athletes engage in activities that bring them positive emotion (e.g., watching funny movies). There is an interesting finding called "the undoing effect of positive emotions" (Branigan et al. 2000). Participants in a study whose attention was turned toward a cheerful movie recovered from negative emotions (rumination and worry) faster than those who saw either a neutral or sad movie or remained without intervention.

Another method for helping athletes out of a slump is to pair them with a teammate who is doing well, as a mentor or buddy. The goal is to help them express their feelings to a fellow athlete they can relate to. They may be more comfortable discussing their struggles with a teammate than the coach. A teammate who has been through a slump can share experiences and encourage their teammate. The power differential between coach and athlete can sometimes impair an athlete's ability to get what he or she needs or to be completely honest. Indirectly, this also strengthens relationships on the team.

A third idea for helping an athlete out of a slump is to use visualization. Have him or her review in their mind an exceptional performance in their own athletic history. If possible, show him or her film of this performance if you have it. He or she can play their own success tape in their minds again and again. If it relates to hitting the ball in baseball or softball, have him or her see himself or herself hitting the ball, hear the sound of the crack of the bat on the ball, smell the air, and visualize the arc of the ball flying through the air. He or she might hear the sounds of people cheering, their teammates, or the sounds of their feet running around the bases. The more sensory input, the better: see it, hear it, feel it, smell it. Jason Selk, in *10-Minute Toughness,* calls it the "personal performance reel" (2009).

Suinn (1972, 1984) has had athletes do visual motor behavioral rehearsal (VMBR). In his method, skiers run through their downhill courses in their mind, and he has actually seen some firing in the muscles when the skiers imagine the roughest part of the terrain. Obviously, the brain and the body have an ability to imagine the challenges of the course. Many elite-level athletes use visualization, and while the research is not conclusive, it clearly can get athletes thinking about their routines and skills. It has also been suggested that imaginal experiences—that is, seeing something in our minds—can increase self-efficacy, or our belief in our ability to do a certain task (Maddux 2005). One important caveat is that athletes need to be able to see their positive or best performances, not their mistakes. If they cannot imagine themselves successfully performing, visualization may not be helpful (Williams and Krane 2015).

Lastly, help an athlete who is in a slump focus on task and process, rather than outcome. Stop the athlete from exclusively focusing on outcomes (e.g., hits, free-throw shots made, total shots, goals). Have him or her focus on working their skill and becoming more consistent through practice and repetition. If their technique is solid, then suggest a cue word or short phrase that relates to process or strategy; for example, with batting, "Relax; smooth swing."

Coaching Tips for Slumps

- Focus on what the athlete's strengths are. Have him or her list their strengths, and build him or her up by emphasizing those strengths, with trust and expectation that the slump will pass.

- Have him or her make a practice of writing in an athletic journal about what went right and what he or she is thankful for (at least three things, but the more the better).

- Pair him or her with a teammate who has been through a slump before and has gotten past it. Ask the teammate to support and share with the athlete what he or she learned from that time.

- Your athlete may need repeated reminders to relax and trust the process. Suggest a phrase that he or she can repeat, such as "trust yourself." Ask the athlete what he or she does to relax.

- Encourage the athlete to do repeated visualization of best-performance situations. Have him or her run through this "performance reel" (Selk 2009) in their mind repeatedly. I prefer to have athletes do this outside of practice times, such as before going to sleep at night or when waking. The key is they must repeat this frequently.

- Have the athlete focus on task mastery and repeated practice of essential skills. Try to get him or her out of evaluating himself or herself based on outcome alone (e.g., number of shots made, successful hits). Encourage him or her to remain steady in their practice with faith in the process.

Chapter 10

MIND-SET

You are watching your team practice hitting in the batting cages at the gym. You hear a player talking to her teammate as she leaves the batting cage. "I can never hit the ball when she throws a low ball," she tells her fellow batter. Her teammate encourages her, "Just keep at it. I couldn't hit them for a while. You can do it if you keep working at it." You recognize that the first player's attitude will never help her hit the low ball. But what do you say to her? How do you help her think like the teammate who told her to keep working at it?

As a coach, you are interested in teaching your players attitudes that help them learn their skills and work hard at their craft. This chapter will discuss research on mind-set, a concept that has been developed in the past ten to fifteen years and has an impact on how we learn, whether we stick with things over time, and how we deal with challenges and adversity. According to research, we can teach this mind-set.

If Carol Dweck listened to the dialogue between the players above, she would suggest that these players have a difference in mind-set. She has spent a number of years researching and writing about a *growth mind-set* versus a *fixed mind-set*. These terms from Dweck's research at Stanford University are explained in a book called *Mindset: The New Psychology of Success* (2006). In her book, she describes the differences between the two types of mind-set and says a growth mind-set can be taught. The difference in this pattern of thinking can greatly influence an individual's effort, and as a result, she has related it to sport performance. Finally, which mind-set we adopt influences how we explain our successes and failures, and influences our approach to tasks.

Winning with Growth Mind-Set

In simple terms, an individual with a growth mind-set approaches problems and challenges differently than an individual with a fixed mind-set. An athlete who is working on a three-point shot who has a growth mind-set thinks, "I can't do it now, but I am working toward being able to do this," whereas an athlete with a fixed mind-set thinks, "I'll never be good at this!" One attitude inspires hard work and effort, whereas the other causes an athlete to quit when frustrated. In the perspective of fixed mind-set, talent is finite; comparatively, in the growth mind-set, there are no limits to what an athlete can learn if he or she is willing to work hard. Talent is built on hard work and effort. How is it that some athletes seem to have this attitude in their makeup while others don't? If we believe that mental toughness can be taught, then we will work toward a growth mind-set attitude in all of our athletes.

Some of the characteristics of athletes with a growth mind-set are that they will learn from their experiences, embrace challenges, persist in the face of difficulty, and see effort as the road to mastery (Dweck 2006). When criticized, an individual with a growth mind-set will learn from feedback. Criticism is viewed as an opportunity to improve. How athletes view criticism is vital to how coachable they are. Helping athletes not to personalize criticism but to see it as an opportunity for growth is important.

When an athlete takes criticism personally, you can see it in his or her face. He or she wears a look of shame or disappointment. He or she is feeling rather than thinking. Practicing a phrase like, "I am not sure I can do it now, but I can learn to with time, effort, and persistence," will help him or her to connect with a growth mind-set. Talk to your athletes about the purpose of criticism. Its purpose is to help them improve, not put them down. Teaching athletes to recognize that they have a choice in how they receive criticism can set them up for interpreting criticism from their coaches in a helpful manner.

In addition, their responses to errors during competition can be changed. Teaching an athlete a phrase like, "mistakes are opportunities to learn," can create simple shifts in automatic responses to behaviors, which help build a growth mind-set.

If you would like to learn more about your own mind-set, you can take a short survey questionnaire at: http://mindsetonline.com/testyourmindset/step1.php.

Another example is if an athlete fails a speed test, the player with the growth mind-set considers that he or she has a lot of work to do. The player with the fixed mind-set thinks, *Why bother working at this, as I never seem to pass this speed test*. Athletes may actually *avoid* challenges or situations where they do not show skill or show weakness, since they believe it is inevitable that they will fail. This leads to a dead end because the athlete with this mind-set plateaus. Again, he or she sees talent as finite or inborn rather than earned from hard work.

Developing a Growth Mind-Set

How do teams develop a growth mind-set? I believe coaches are integral to modeling this mind-set, sharing hope with a developing team by focusing on weak areas and developing those skills, and by continuously emphasizing and praising effort and hard work. Failure is responded to with, "We have more work to do," or, "We needed to work harder today in order to beat that team," or, "That team put out more effort and has a higher skill level than we do right now." Notice the implication that nothing is set in stone and that hard work leads to success. Your language as a coach conveys your own attitude about growth.

Dale Brown, the most successful basketball coach in LSU history, with 426 wins, stated: "I pretty much say the same thing for a tough loss as for a good win. I always tell them that it's not the I.Q. of a person I'm interested in, but the F.Q. (failure quotient) of a person" (Brennan 1995).

The failure quotient, according to Brown, was the ability to successfully bounce back from adversity. As coaches, you are well aware that failures occur within the game and between games, many times over the course of a season (Brennan 1995). A growth mind-set on the part of the coach and the players helps to establish a high FQ.

Coaching Tips for Growth Mind-Set

- It means that you ask questions concerning how they are *thinking* about their skills.
  "I hear you stating that you will never be able to hit those low balls. I disagree. I think if you work your tail off and focus your practice, you will get better. It depends on you and how much effort and work you are willing to put in."
- It means that you regularly ask how hard they are willing to work to accomplish X goal.
  "How important is it to you to develop as a team? How badly do you want to go to conference play? Are you willing to put in the time, in practice and outside of practice?"
- Ask your players, "Can you believe that even if you cannot do X skill today, you are working in the direction of it? How badly would you like to learn to hit those low balls? Are you willing to direct your practice toward that goal? How can our coaching staff help you reach that goal?"
- It means you praise effort, not outcome. It also means you link wins and successes to hard work.
  "I am really impressed by how hard you all worked at today's practice. Your effort on shooting really showed. I see improvements." Or, "While we didn't

win today, we fought hard. We scored more runs, fielded better than last game, and you all kept fighting until the end." Your language as a coach can reflect a growth mind-set: "Today we have a big challenge before us. I am interested in your best effort to work hard together. Let's focus on playing more aggressively than we did last game."

- If you notice an athlete apparently disappointed in his or her performance, or beating himself or herself up in the head (he or she looks disgusted, head down, eyes down, muttering under his or her breath), talk to him or her about his or her thoughts. Help them *think*. "What can you learn from this for the next game?" Emphasize that they can focus their practice in this area as they work toward their goal.

Chapter 11

PARENTS AND TECHNOLOGY

You are sitting in your office before a practice, eating your lunch and checking emails. Surprisingly, you see an email from one of your sophomore player's parents. Reading through the email, you feel the heat rising in you; you can't believe the father of this athlete is taking issue with something you said to his daughter yesterday. You are thinking that this never would have happened back in your playing days. Who the heck does this guy think he is? Emailing a college coach? You wonder if this athlete has any idea that her dad is getting in the middle of some critical but constructive feedback you shared with this young woman.

Your next thought is, *What do I do with this? Do I respond?* You decide that you are not going to do anything at the moment, because you are ticked off, and it may not come across very well. Taking some time to think about it is best. Maybe your assistant coach can help. *Should I talk to the team about this? I don't want to embarrass the player.* Parents can contact you; you just don't want them interfering with coaching.

Dilemmas like the one above happen more frequently these days as college kids have more frequent contact with their parents than in previous generations. This chapter will discuss issues coaches face in dealing with athletes' parents; it will also explore the impact of technology on communication between athletes and parents, as well as coaches and team members.

Digital Natives

Working with college students for the past twenty years, I have found some significant differences in the amount of contact young people have with their parents compared to those of us who were raised in the sixties and seventies. In my classes, students have engaged in a number of discussions about the use of cell phones and the impact on their communication with parents. I am fascinated by how technology affects young adults' development of independence from their parents. I am also the parent of two college-aged children and have made some deliberate decisions about contact with my kids while they are away at school.

One of the most interesting discussions I had in the classroom took place about eight years ago among a group of students in my psychology class at George Mason. One student spoke of finding it restrictive to have to call or text his mother every time he traveled. I asked him to give an example. He said he went away for a weekend trip with a couple friends to a beach resort while he was at school. He mentioned it to his mother, and she insisted that he let her know when he arrived and when he was leaving. The student reflected that his mother would not have known about it or worried about it if he hadn't mentioned it to her. He yearned for more independence from his parents while at school.

Another student who was married and in her midtwenties shared that she called home at ten o'clock every evening. It was just a check-in call to share the day's events. I was surprised that she did this, as she was married, and I wondered how her spouse felt about this. The student then revealed that she became anxious whenever she could not reach her parents, and she felt heightened anxiety until she heard from them. Clearly, this was a way of keeping in touch with her parents and something she enjoyed. But this student, contrary to the first student, found it hard *not* to have daily contact. The variety of norms among students in this one class regarding cell phone contact with parents impressed me as an issue that has a significant impact on young adults' development of emotional independence.

Discussions like these, as well as my discussion with clients in my practice, started me thinking about the behavioral impact of cell phones. Texting has become one of the primary modes of communication with friends, dating relationships, and parents; it has changed how young people communicate. By its very nature, a text is ambiguous at times. Tone of voice, humor, and nuance can be lost in a text. Oftentimes, young people express concern or confusion about the meaning of a text communication. In addition, because of the instantaneous nature of texts and cell phone calls, these wonderful communication devices are potentially anxiety inducing.

Parents of teens often worry if they do not hear back from their kids. Sometimes, students may feel worry about their loved ones if they cannot reach them. Making contact with loved ones and receiving this instant satisfaction or relief can become highly reinforcing and therefore create a dependency. So if students or their parents cannot reach each other, they may become anxious until they do. Some students actually talk to their parents or text them every day. Coaches also use texting to let athletes know about schedule changes or other team information. It is a good idea to avoid any loaded or emotional communication via text. It is frequently misinterpreted because it lacks tone of voice and facial communication; save important messages for face-to-face talks with your team.

Technology has significantly influenced this generation of kids, who have been called "digital natives" (Prensky 2001). Most of our college students were babies after cell phones became prevalent in our culture. The majority of them acquired cell phones as tweens or young teenagers. They navigated preadolescence with instant messaging and adolescence with the use of a cell phone, contacting friends via text messaging; later they used Instagram, Facebook, Snapchat, or Twitter. They are incredibly savvy when it comes to communication in short, cryptic messages and pictures. They are also used to receiving rapid feedback from friends and parents. Often, they consult with friends or parents when making decisions because it is quick and easy.

As a consequence of this frequent contact, I believe our young adults' ability to function independently has been significantly affected. How many of us rely exclusively on ourselves to make certain decisions? Often we take pictures of potential purchases, share scenes from our experiences, post images to Facebook, or simply text our significant others with questions to consider their thoughts. Many older adults are puzzled by their middle-aged kids' and grandkids' constant use of and obsession with their phones. (Although lately I have seen quite a few older adults staring at their screens! My dad, who is almost eighty, reads quite a bit of news and books on his phone.) In terms of contact with college kids, most parents enjoy the ability to have frequent information and feedback about how their sons or daughters are doing at school. This is no less true of our athletes. Lots of parents follow their athlete sons and daughters on Facebook, Twitter, and Instagram. I have found these helpful when I am away from teams I am working with during their competitions. Many teams post the progress during their games on Twitter.

How does this influence the coaching of our young athletes? Consider that parents, close friends, and former coaches are seconds away through text and social media. This means that an athlete can discuss feedback from a coach on the spot with their parents, friends, or others. When the coach delivers critical feedback that a player does not receive well, this can cause discomfort. Athletes might reach out to a significant person in their circle of guidance to help them cope with it or to discuss it. Because of this, the athlete may not have to struggle with the feedback and think it over. He or she may also not ask the coach to discuss it. Another potential outcome is that others' input may dilute the impact of the feedback if a parent or former coach contradicts the coach's feedback. Coaches have shared with me that this is sometimes a challenge of coaching today's young athletes.

Tact and Diplomacy

In addition, coaches have shared that they have received phone calls or emails from parents questioning their decisions about their athletes—even college athletes. For example, their son or daughter may not be getting playing time, and the parent may call to share their feelings about this with the coach. This can be quite challenging. First, a parent may not show respect for the coach. Second, it sends a message to their young adult athlete that he or she does not need to accept the coach's decisions. Third, it can interfere with an athlete's relationship with his or her coach. Obviously, this is not true of all athletes or their parents. Some parents encourage their young adult athletes to deal with their coaches directly, encouraging them to communicate, ask questions, and face conflicts directly. Because they have had the ability to access their parents' input so easily, however, many young adult students are not as capable of managing these situations independently as we were forced to do in earlier years, simply because our parents were less involved or available by phone.

At a conference a couple of years ago, an academic dean of a major college in Virginia shared with me that she was troubled by the level of entitlement that many parents had regarding their college kids. She mentioned that she was often contacted by parents who would try to negotiate on their kids' behalf. She added that dealing with parents today was a challenging part of her job that didn't exist ten to fifteen years ago. When teaching a psychology class a couple years ago, I was quite surprised to receive an email from a concerned parent about her son's poor grades in my class. I had to inform her that I could not talk to her directly, as it was a violation of our rules, since he is not a minor and the university does not treat him as such.

So how can a coach deal with this issue directly or indirectly with student athletes and their parents? If you are working at the high school level or with travel league players, it is more straightforward. Having a parents' handbook with guidelines about communication, expectations for parental input into coaching decisions, and the level of contact they can expect between coaches and parents can help to establish rules around this issue.

At the college level, it is more complex, as the NCAA has rules for parents. Coaches need to address these issues up front with their student athletes. Let athletes know that if they have issues, you would like them to deal with you directly, as opposed to going through their parents. In addition, it might be helpful to inform them that you hope that they would take your feedback and process it on their own before instantly sharing it with their parents or others in their life. Try to establish the idea of trust in working with you as a coach, and encourage student athletes to come to you and discuss feedback if they have a legitimate problem. You can also give them examples of the type of problem you want to hear about or discuss with them, to help them differentiate between big problems and small problems. This encouragement to communicate on their own is so important for college-aged students. We have to teach our young adults to deal with issues and conflicts with their future bosses or authority figures directly, rather than circuitously. If an athlete has an issue he or she is struggling with and it involves you, establishing a norm of open, direct communication will develop an increased level of trust on the team.

Understandably, if a coach is acting in a way that is inappropriate, then athletes need to let someone know. There are staff members within the athletic department of a university or college who have a designated role to help with these kinds of problems. But coaches may need to ask athletes for some consideration with regard to their coaching relationships with athletes. Teams are much like families, and honoring the boundaries around communication and behavior on the particular team is important.

Some specific suggestions for youth-level coaches are offered in the book *Successful Coaching* by Rainer Martens (2014).

Have a parent-orientation meeting with these suggested topics:

- Introduce yourself.
- Explain your coaching philosophy.
- Explain potential risks.
- Explain specifics of your program.

- Explain athlete policies (these can be covered in a handbook).
- Explain parent policies.

In *Successful Coaching*, Martens also suggests the following parental guidelines:

- Remain in the spectator area.
- Let the coach be the coach.
- Provide only supportive comments to coaches, officials, and athletes of both teams. Avoid derogatory comments.
- Do not coach your son or daughter during the game or contest.
- Do not drink alcohol at practice or contests or come after having drunk too much.
- Cheer for your team.
- Show interest, enthusiasm, and support for your athlete.
- Control your emotions.
- Help when asked by coaches or officials (Martens 2014).

My suggestions for guidelines for coaches who are dealing with college-level athletes are as follows:

- Acknowledge the importance of your athletes' relationships with parents.
- Encourage your athlete to deal with you as coach directly instead of always discussing issues with parents, friends, or former coaches if they have a problem.

- If they have a major conflict with you, and they do not feel they can talk to you about it, they should seek out an appropriate staff member in the athletic department.
- Encourage your athlete to take in feedback and try to work with it constructively.
- Discuss the use of technology and its impact on your communication with athletes, stating your preferences or norms for communication (e.g., do you text changes to practices, use email, etc.).
- Encourage athletes to pick their battles, recognizing that coaches are human, make mistakes, and have bad days.

Coaching Tips for Parents and Technology

- Because of technology, parents have more frequent contact with the majority of students today. They also are major stakeholders in their young athlete's success.
- Discuss your expectations with the team regarding communication with parents.
- Establish norms early on in a team's life and provide guidelines for your athletes with regard to your use of technology.
- Encourage athletes to talk to you directly if they have a problem with you.
- Try to keep an attitude of openness, sincerity, and trust to keep these channels of communication open with your athletes.

Chapter 12

ACADEMIC PERFORMANCE

You are sitting in your office when the phone rings. The caller ID says it is from the academic coordinator in the athletic department. "Coach, bad news. Connor can't play this spring. He's failing two subjects, and his GPA is too low."

Choice words float through your head. How can this guy, who is so brilliant on the field, not pay attention to something you know he can do? How do you convince him to do the work when you never have to urge him to do the work in practice? You feel the frustration rising, knowing that your team is going to be compromised without him.

What's interesting to you as a coach is that only a handful of your athletes are as serious about their academics as they are about their sports. They are achievement oriented and do not require anyone to push them. They push themselves, managing their time on and off the field and in the gym. Academic performance among athletes is among the major concerns for college and high school coaches. NCAA rules require a certain grade point average in order to play, and often athletes fall short of this. Retention of athletes in college is also an issue, with some athletes failing out of school. Athletic directors around the country seek to understand what helps athletes handle the heavy demands of sports while also staying on top of their courses and grades. This chapter will focus on what you can do as the coach to help your athletes be successful in the classroom, as well as helping them to develop their professional interests beyond college.

Fostering Learning

The likelihood that high school and/or college athletes will go on to play professionally is slim. Thus, most of these young men and women will need something to fall back on. Their competitive sport life may be finished at the end of their high school or college years. Colleges and universities know that and spend a lot of effort trying to ensure that their athletes get the help they need to be successful academically.

Academic success is similar to athletic success in some key ways: they both require excellent time management, discipline, and self-regulation. Budgeting time, which is scarce for college athletes, is one of the challenges. It means delaying gratification of immediate wants or needs and working at long-term goals. It's about self-regulation. What is self-regulation? It's an ability to divide up tasks and work at them steadily. It also involves the ability to monitor yourself and do things you don't want to do. Athletes are generally people who love to move; they hate to sit still, and schoolwork almost always involves sitting still and focusing on reading, studying, doing problem sets, or writing papers. Not exactly a first-choice activity to those who love to move! Using mindfulness skills like the brief centering exercise and the mindful breathing exercise (Gardner and Moore 2007) can be a helpful means of releasing tension and focusing attention. (See chapter 7, "Arousal and Anxiety," for mindfulness exercises.) Many students in my classes have reported to me that these simple exercises done at the beginning of class help them to concentrate on the material presented, clearing their minds of what they just finished doing. A number of them use it before they study, in order to better focus their attention.

Some of the coaches I work with have incredible dedication to building strength, speed, and stamina or developing skills over time. As a coach, you know getting good grades in school requires the same type of process; it's just a different venue. A coach can support academic success by talking about it and valuing it. Let your team know how important it is that they learn and succeed in school. Remind them that most of them will go on to work jobs after college or graduate school. Most high schools, colleges, and universities recognize scholar athletes in some fashion. But coaches can create their own brand of academic support by rewarding personal improvement. This requires some work in keeping track of grades and increases in academic performance. As a coach, you can draw attention to successes and talk about how intelligence on and off the field or court is highly valuable. Can you as a coach come up with some recognitions midsemester and end of semester when grades are recorded? This can be especially helpful for the newer players (e.g., freshmen and sophomores) because one wants to set standards high early on. Isn't that what excellence and mastery are all about—setting the bar high and working in small increments in the direction of valued goals?

As a coach, you can also encourage a love of learning, since this is truly helpful. Asking athletes how important it is for them to be successful academically is also helpful. The acceptance and commitment therapy (ACT) approach often focuses individuals on their values and asks people what they are willing to do (or not do) in order to reach those goals (Harris and Hayes 2009). It can also be beneficial to ask them who can help them reach their goals. In the same way that you help your players outline athletic skills goals (or mental goals), you can ask them to outline their academic goals for the semester. Asking athletes what they need to start (or stop) doing can be a useful method to figuring out behaviors that need to be added or taken away (e.g., procrastinating on term papers; failing to go to extra review sessions; texting or using social media while studying) (Gardner and Moore 2007). This all comes from an excellent book called *The Psychology of Enhancing Human Performance: The Mindfulness-Acceptance-Commitment Approach*, by Frank Gardner and Zella Moore (2007). They have designed a seven-week program that focuses athletes on these questions and has handouts to support the work.

Carol Dweck's work on mind-set is also something to consider in the light of academic achievement (Dweck 2006). (See chapter 10, "Growth Mind-Set versus Fixed Mind-Set.") She studies motivation and achievement in children and young adults. The belief that intelligence or ability is finite is what she calls the "entity theory." Belief that we only have so much ability can get in the way of putting forth effort. Entity theory is similar to some athletes' views of their athletic skill as inborn talent, not something that can be improved upon with dedication over time. On the other hand, if we believe that intelligence is something that we can increase with effort (according to her "incremental" perspective), we are more likely to work at achieving our learning goals. Daniel Pink, in the book *Drive* (2009), explains it well.

> If you believe intelligence is a fixed quantity, then every educational and professional encounter becomes a measure of how much you have. If you believe intelligence is something you can increase, then the same encounters become opportunities for growth. (Pink 2009)

Unfortunately, in the academic domain, many athletes carry with them the belief that they are not good at school. This belief hurts them when they attempt mastery in the classroom. Likening school to strength or athletic skill can be helpful to them, since they have the mastery experiences in the gym. They simply need to see the process of reaching goals in the classroom in the same way. Dweck has also demonstrated that students who are asked to learn something to increase their understanding, rather than to get a good grade, will work longer and try more solutions when given a novel challenge (Dweck 1999). Thus, the two different styles of thinking seem to prompt different responses to difficulty. One is the helpless response, and the other is mastery oriented (Dweck 1999).

Another method to help athletes stay focused on what they are trying to achieve in school is to teach them methods of self-regulation. Instructing them in keeping a calendar of assignments, using their cell phones to set up reminder cues to work on tasks, monitoring their own progress, and directing their thoughts and will in ways that help them to work toward goals can help develop a process. The use of affirming thoughts can be effective; for example, "I can become even better at biology if I spend the time regularly and study hard." These thoughts open us up to the possibilities of changing behaviors.

Asking athletes to talk about their academic goals and what they want to do after graduation can help them to connect with their own motivation. If they don't have a clear goal beyond graduation, they may need direction. Some teams offer athletes experiences like personality and career testing, such as the Clifton Strengths Finder. Go to the link to learn more about this test: http://strengthstest.com/strengthsfinderthemes/strengths-themes.html.

Encourage your athletes who are uncertain about what they want to do after graduation to talk to their teachers or professors in classes they like; they can also contact people in the community who do jobs they think they might be interested in. Just as they worked toward playing sports in high school or college, they can work at finding a major they enjoy. Many departments offer career fairs to help students learn more about professions in their specialty area. You are simply encouraging them to be whole people while also being athletes, and continuously reminding them of the rapidity of their school athletic careers. Many students reflect on the fact that they are surprised by how quickly their educational years pass.

Another idea is to bring in former college athletes who successfully made the transition into the job world and have them talk about it with your team. How did they deal with the academic challenges during their college athletic career? What advice would they share with your athletes? Asking them to talk about their experiences of finishing their competitive sport life and moving into a career can also be enlightening to your athletes. Anything that helps them connect with their futures and lets them know that what they do now in the academic realm affects their options later will have the potential to motivate them. Although many athletes head into a profession that connects with their athletic life (e.g., coaching, sports management, physical therapy, etc.), others go into professions where sport will no longer be at the forefront of their existence. A few years ago, a student who was a college soccer player confided in me as she approached graduation that she had played soccer since she was four years old, and she was feeling a lot of stress about losing this vital part of herself. How can coaches help athletes make this transition? Having them talk about this in the team setting might be helpful.

Here are some questions that often assist students to work harder toward their goals:

- Why are you in school?
- Who has encouraged you to go to college? Who cares the most about how well you do academically? Why?

- Who can support you in working toward getting good grades?
- Why will you feel good if you succeed in school?
- Do you approach your classes with the same initiative and motivation as your sport? Why or why not?
- Do you believe that you have the ability to get better at academics, or do you believe that your ability is limited? Where have those beliefs come from, and are they helpful to you at this point in your life?

Ideas for activities that can help students connect with their academic goals:

- Have students discuss their goals beyond college and sports. What do they see themselves doing in five years or ten years? Do they know anyone who is doing that now? Can they talk to people who are engaged in doing the job they see themselves pursuing?
- Share the services offered at your college or university's career-counseling department (or career center in high school). Find out if there are career tests available to your athletes and help them to consider taking them for their own self-knowledge.
- Set up some form of self-monitoring system with athletes and their academic performance. Do not consider grades alone but also effort and improvement. Check in with your players during the semester. Encourage them to keep track of how they are doing.

- Consider rewarding the top three students on your team (e.g., highest GPA) and the three most improved GPAs with some sort of acknowledgment.
- Invite a former player who has been out of school for a few years to come and talk to your team about his or her work. Ask him or her to talk about their college athletic career, the challenges he or she faced, and what he or she learned.

Coaching Tips for Academic Performance

- Communicate how important their academic performance is to you as their coach.
- Ask athletes probing questions about why school is important to them. If they say it is not, encourage others who do value school to share why.
- Set up some form of recognition system to mark success in your athletes' academic performance.
- Teach them to apply a growth mind-set to their studies. Make it behavioral by asking them what they would do (or stop doing) to achieve their goals in school.
- Teach them to use self-regulation strategies like calendars and time-management strategies.
- Foster interest in their future careers. Bring graduated athletes in to talk about life after college sports. Encourage them to attend career fairs and learn all they can about their interests.

Closing

Coaching is a set of behaviors and patterns that you have learned and practiced for some time. Many of you have been coaching for years. My goal with this book is to help you use psychological skills to build better teams that can reach higher levels of performance. Every team enjoys winning more than losing, but many things go into building winning teams. By learning concepts in psychology and trying some of these practices, my goal is for you to be able to be an even more effective coach who can lead your teams to even greater success.

I enjoy empowering people to be more successful in their various roles in life. Coaches face a lot of pressure, especially at the higher levels. College sports bring big money to universities and colleges, and athletic directors want coaches who can produce winning teams. The demands to win are significant and real. The process of building teams takes time and patience, however. Both the skills and the relationships with players are key components of this work.

Even high school coaches face pressure. Often they are developing future talent for college teams, and parents want to see results. Parents pay travel and club team coaches well and expect to see growth in their young athletes. Developing yourself as a coach is a worthwhile goal.

A dean of an education school once told me that we start and end with ourselves in the classroom (as teachers). I believe this is true on the field and in the gym. We bring our personalities, our personal and family history, our athletic history, and our work history to the gym with us each day. This book is not intended for you to change who you are but to make you think, consider the effects of your own behavior with your teams, and give you ideas of things you can do to foster the development of cohesion on your team.

The first few chapters of this book focused on communication, motivation, and goal setting. The specialty area of positive psychology has studied positive communication in families, organizations, and groups and has demonstrated the impact positivity can have on athletic and academic performance and function. Creating strong groups that communicate well on and off the field or court helps build winning teams. Communication is the bedrock and occurs between head coaches, assistants, and trainers, as well as between coaches and athletes. These are fundamental to coaching. Try incorporating some of these practices into your coaching to improve what you do. Becoming an authoritative coach who communicates well and knows how to motivate athletes could improve your work.

Building group cohesion on your team will help the team climate and get the athletes working more effectively together, and it is more than simply team-building games. Many experiences on teams contribute to the sense of cohesion. The activities in chapter 6, "Team Cohesion," can help to facilitate the development of cohesion. Winning teams are more cohesive than teams that are less successful. Thus, coaches who are in the process of helping a team to develop over a couple of seasons have a greater challenge to help create cohesive experiences. Doing team-building games and exercises like those listed in chapter 6 can help to establish cohesion. Not enough coaches take the time to build the team group or attend to the changes in the team's group over the course of the season. My experience is that changes in the group can inhibit top performance. Team building and dealing with group dynamics has long been a part of what business coaches recommend to managers to increase productivity and morale. If there are problems among your team members, you should address them.

Throughout this book I have tried to bring in relevant research and practices that increase present-moment attention. Mindfulness, covered in the chapter on anxiety and arousal (chapter 7), is one of the key practices that can positively impact athletes' ability to stay focused. Incorporating these exercises and practices into your team's preparation will help develop this mental skill in your teams. The mindfulness exercises do not have to be long. Five to seven minutes can make a huge difference in quieting the mind and bringing an athlete into the here and now. Some of the programs that have been developed for sports use longer exercises. My experience is that it's most effective to start small and increase slowly. Chapter 7 also describes techniques for helping athletes to know their bodies and offers tools to empower them to adjust their arousal levels to improve performance. Chapters 8 and 9 consider choking and slumps, as well as ways that you, as a coach, can practice to help reduce the likelihood of choking in competition.

Chapter 10 on mind-set was an addition that I debated for some time. Adopting a growth mind-set in challenging endeavors (including sports) can be life changing and create a compassion for self that is often lacking in the athletic world. Carol Dweck's work has broad influences in terms of sports and performance. I hope that you will feel inclined to read her work directly.

Chapter 11, "Dealing with Parents and the Impact of Technology," grew out of conversations with students, coaches, and my work with clients. Technology has major impacts on the way we communicate, and this has significant effects on athletes and coaches. The amount of contact students have today with their parents is higher during the college years than in previous generations. As a result, coaches' decisions and behaviors are often discussed with parents; occasionally, parents contact coaches, and this is at times an awkward situation for a coach. Discussion in that chapter gives some ideas of ways to manage that process.

And last, chapter 12 focuses on academics, which is something that many coaches don't like to have to deal with but is a very real part of college success among athletes. Whether athletes can play or not depends on their achievement academically. Teams establish specific people whose sole job it is to monitor athlete academic progress. Consider trying some of the strategies in this chapter to bolster your athletes' success academically.

Finally, I hope that some of the ideas in this book will compel you to take better care of yourself, since you are the instrument of the work you do as a coach. Coaching is demanding work, not unlike teaching, parenting, and human service work. When you are tired or strung out, your voice and demeanor will reflect it. Our modeling of mindfulness, or present-moment awareness, as well as focusing on the here and now, is critical for athletes to witness. Your composure and human capacity for handling things well under pressure can have a huge impact on your team.

Coaches, I wish you all the best in your work to develop high-performing athletes and teams! Please feel free to contact me at www.mindfulathleticperformance.com.

References

Bandura, A. 1997. *Self-efficacy: The exercise of control.* New York: W. H. Freeman.

Bartholomew, K. J., N. Ntoumanis, R. M. Ryan, J. A. Bosch, and C. Thogersen-Ntoumani. 2011. "Self-determination theory and diminished functioning: The role of interpersonal control and psychological need thwarting." *Personality and Social Psychology Bulletin* 37: 1459–1473.

Baumrind, D. 1966. "Effects of authoritative parental control on child behavior." *Child Development* 37 (4): 887–907.

——— 1991. "The influence of parenting style on adolescent competence and substance use." *Journal of Early Adolescence* 11 (1): 56–95.

Beauchamp, M. R., S. R. Bray, M. A. Eys, and A. V. Carron. 2002. "Role ambiguity, role efficacy, and role performance: Multidimensional and mediational relationships within interdependent sport teams." *Group Dynamics: Theory, Research and Practice* 6: 229–242.

Beck, A. T., A. J. Rush, B. F. Shaw, and G. Emery. 1979. *Cognitive Therapy of Depression*. New York: Guilford Press.

Beilock, S. L. 2010. *Choke: What the Secrets of the Brain Reveal About Getting It Right When You Have To*. New York: Free Press.

Beilock S. L., T. H. Carr, C. MacMahon, and J. L. Starkes. 2002. "When paying attention becomes counterproductive: Impact of divided versus skill-focused attention on novices and experienced performance of sensorimotor skills." *Journal of Experimental Psychology: Applied* 8: 6–16.

Bilas, J. 2013. *Toughness: Developing True Strength On and Off the Court*. New York: Penguin Group.

Branch, J. 2009. "For free throws, fifty years of practice is no help." http://www.nytimes.com/2009/03/04/sports/basketball/04freethrow.html.

Branigan, C., B. L. Fredrickson, R. A. Mancuso, and M. M. Tugade. 2000. "The undoing effect of positive emotions." *Motivation and Emotion* 24: 237–58.

Brennan, S. J. 1995. *Competitive Excellence: The Psychology and Strategy of Successful Team Building*. Omaha: Peak Performance Publishing.

———. 1991. "The influence of parenting styles on adolescent competence and substance use." Journal of Early Adolescence 11 (1:1): 56–95.

Brody, J. E. 2007. "Mental reserves keep brain agile." New York Times (December 11). Retrieved from http://www.nytimes.com.

Cameron, K. 2012. *Positive Leadership: Strategies for Extraordinary Performance.* San Francisco: Berrett-Koehler Publishers.

Carron, A. V., L. R. Brawley, and W. N. Widmeyer. 1998. "The Measurement of Cohesiveness in Sport Groups." In *Advancements in Sport and Exercise Psychology Measurement,* edited by J. L. Duda. Morgantown: Fitness Information Technology.

Carron, A. V., and M. A. Eys. 2012. *Group Dynamics in Sport,* 4th ed. Morgantown: Fitness Information Technology.

The Clifton Strengths Finder assessment: http://strengthstest.com/strengthsfinderthemes/strengths-themes.html.

Cuddy, Amy. "Your body language shapes who you are." TED video 21:02. Filmed June 2012. Posted 2012. https://www.ted.com/talks/amy_cuddy_your_body_language_shapes_who_you_are.

Darling, N. 1999. *Parenting Style and Its Correlates.* Champaign: ERIC Clearinghouse on Elementary and Early Childhood Education.

Davis, H., M. Liotti, E. T. Ngan, T. S. Woodward, J. X. Van Snellenberg, S. M. van Anders, A. Smith, and H.

Mayberg. 2008. "fMRI bold signal changes in elite swimmers while viewing videos of personal failure." *Brain Imaging and Behavior* 2: 84–93.

———— 1999. Self-Theories: Their Role in Motivation, Personality and Development. Philadelphia: Psychology Press.

Dweck, C. 2006. Mindset: The New Psychology of Success. New York: Ballantine.

Emmons, R. A. and M. E. McCullough. 2003. "Counting blessings versus burdens: An experimental investigation of gratitude and subjective well being in daily life." *Journal of Personality and Social Psychology* 84: 377–89.

Eys, M. A., J. Hardy, A. V. Carron, and M. R. Beauchamp. 2003. "The relationship between task cohesion and competitive state anxiety." *Journal of Sport and Exercise Psychology* 25: 66–76.

Fredrickson, B. L. 2009. *Positivity: Top-Notch Research Reveals the 3:1 Ratio That Will Change Your Life.* New York: Three Rivers Press.

Gagne, M., R. M. Ryan, and K. Bargmann. 2003. "Autonomy support and need satisfaction in the motivation and well-being of gymnasts." *Journal of Applied Sport Psychology* 15: 372–390.

Gallimore, R., and R. Tharp. 2004. "What a coach can teach a teacher 1975–2004: Reflections and reanalysis of John Wooden's teaching practices." *Sport Psychologist* 18 (2): 119–137.

Gardner, F. L., and Z. Moore. 2007. *The Psychology of Enhancing Human Performance: The Mindfulness-Acceptance-Commitment (MAC) Approach.* New York: Springer Publishing.

Gould, D., R. C. Eklund, and S. A. Jackson. 1992a. "1988 U.S. Olympic wrestling excellence: I. Mental preparation, precompetitive cognition and effect." *Sport Psychologist* 6: 383–402.

Gould, D., R. C. Eklund, and S. A. Jackson. 1992b. "1988 U.S. wrestling excellence: II. Thoughts and effect occurring during competition." *Sport Psychologist* 6: 383–402.

Gould, D., K. Hodge, K. Peterson, and J. Gianni. 1989. "An explanatory examination of strategies used by elite coaches to enhance self-efficacy in athletes." *Journal of Sport and Exercise Psychology* 11: 128–140.

Gray, R. 2004. "Attending to the execution of a complex sensorimotor skill: Expertise differences, choking and slumps." *Journal of Experimental Psychology: Applied* 10: 42–54.

Greenspan, S. 2006. "Rethinking 'harmonious parenting' using a three-factor discipline model." *Child Care in Practice* 12: 5–12.

Hanin, Y. L. 2000. "Successful and Poor Performance and Emotions." In *Emotions in Sport,* edited by Y. L. Hanin, 157–187. Champaign: Human Kinetics.

Hanton, S. and G. Jones. 1999. "The effects of a multimodal intervention program on performers: II Training the butterflies to fly in formation." *Sport Psychologist* 13: 22–41.

Hanton, S., S. Mellalieu, and J. M. Williams. 2015. "Understanding and Managing Stress in Sport." In *Applied Sport Psychology* (7th ed.), edited by J. W. Williams and V. Krane, 207–234. New York: McGraw Hill.

Hardy, J., C. R. Hall, and L. Hardy. 2005. "Quantifying athlete self-talk." *Journal of Applied Sport Psychology* 16: 251–257.

Harris, R. and S. C. Hayes. 2009. *ACT Made Simple: An Easy to Read Primer on Acceptance and Commitment Therapy.* Oakland: New Harbinger.

Hayes, S. C., K. D. Strosahl, and K. G. Wilson. 1999. *Acceptance and Commitment Therapy: An Experiential Approach to Behavior Change.* New York: Guilford Press.

Henderson, J. and O. Owen. 2002. "The 10 greatest chokes in the history of sport." http://www.theguardian.com/observer/osm/story/0,641727,00.html.

Feedback in Athletic Coaching: http://www.sportpsychology today.com/sport-psychology-for-coaches/feedback-in-athletic-coaching-part-1

Feedback in Athletic Coaching, Part 2: http://www.sport psychologytoday.com/sport-psychology-for-coaches/ feedback-in-athletic-coaching-part-2/

Muscle Relaxation: https://www.anxietybc.com/sites/default /files/MuscleRelaxation.pdf.

Jackson, R.C., K. J. Ashford, and G. Norsworthy. 2006. "Attentional focus, dispositional reinvestment and skilled motor performance under pressure." *Journal of Sport and Exercise Psychology* 9: 45–59.

Janssen, J. 1999. *Championship Team Building: What Every Coach Needs to Know to Build a Motivated, Committed and Cohesive Team.* Tucson: The Winning Mind.

Kabat-Zinn, J. 1991. *Full Catastrophe Living: Using the Wisdom of Your Body and Mind to Face Stress, Pain, and Illness.* Bantam Dell in New York NY.

Kaufman, K. A., C. R. Glass, and T. R. Pineau. in press. *Mindful Sport Performance Enhancement: Mental Training for Athletes and Coaches.* Washington, DC: American Psychological Association.

Komaki, J., and F. T. Barnett. 1977. "A behavioral approach to coaching football: Improving the play execution of an offensive backfield on a youth football team." *Journal of Applied Behavioral Analysis* 10: 657–664.

Kraus, M. W., C. Huang, and D. Keltner. 2010. "Tactile communication, cooperation, and performance: An ethological study of the NBA." *Emotion* 10: 745–749.

Krzyzewski, M. 2011. "Coach K on how to connect: To motivate any team, know your audience and tell vivid stories." *Wall Street Journal* (July 16).

Kurkjian, T. "A batting slump can be a scary thing." http://espn.go.com/mlb/story/_/id/7911483/being-slump-feeling-unique-baseball.

Lardon, M. 2008. *Finding Your Zone: Ten Core Lessons for Achieving Peak Performance in Sports and Life.* New York: Penguin Group.

Lewis, C. 1981. "The effects of parental firm control: A reinterpretation of findings." *Psychological Bulletin* 90: 547–563.

Locke, E. A., and G. P. Latham. 1985. "The application of goal setting to sports." *Journal of Sport Psychology* 7: 205–222.

Locke, E. A., and G. P. Latham. 2002. "Building a practically useful theory of goal setting and task motivation: A 35-year odyssey." *American Psychologist* 57: 705–717.

Locke, E. A., K. N. Shaw, L. M. Saari, and G. P. Latham. 1981. "Goal setting and task performance." *Psychological Bulletin* 90: 125–152.

Knight, Kimberly. 2011. "Media Epidemics: Viral Structures in Literature and New Media." PhD diss., University of California, Santa Barbara. MLA International Bibliography. 2013420395.

Longshore, K. M. 2015. "Helping coaches help themselves: The impact of the Mindfulness Training for Coaches (MTC) program on coaching, stress, and emotion management." PhD diss., Temple University, Philadelphia. ProQuest Dissertations Publishing. 3719418.

Lunenburg, F. 2011. "Goal setting theory of motivation." *International Journal of Management, Business and Administration* 15 (1): 1–6.

Maddux, J. E. 2005. "Self-efficacy: The power of believing you can." In *Handbook of Positive Psychology,* edited by C. R Snyder and S. J. Lopez. New York: Oxford University Press.

Martens, R. 2014. *Successful Coaching,* 4th ed. Champaign: Human Kinetics.

McCraty, R., B. Barrios-Choplin, D. Rozman, M. Atkinson, and A. Watkins. 1998. "The impact of a new emotional self-management program on stress, emotions, heart rate variability, DHEA and cortisol." *Integrative Physiological and Behavioral Science* 32: 151–170.

Meichenbaum, D. 1996. "Stress inoculation training for coping with stressors." *Clinical Psychologist* 49: 4–7.

Mumford, G. 2015. *The Mindful Athlete: Secrets to Pure Performance.* Berkeley: Parallax Press.

Pink, D. 2009. *Drive: The Surprising Truth About What Motivates Us.* Boston: Harvard University Press.

Prensky, M. 2001. "Digital natives, digital immigrants." *On the Horizon* 9 (5): 1–6.

Robb, H. 2007. "Values as leading principles in acceptance and commitment therapy." *International Journal of Behavioral Consultation and Therapy* 3 (1): 118–123.

Ryan, R. M., and E. L. Deci. 2007. "An Overview of Self-Determination Theory: An Organismic-Dialectical Perspective." In *Handbook of Self-Determination Research,* edited by E. L. Deci and R. M. Ryan, 3–33. Rochester: University of Rochester Press.

Sage, G. 1984. *Motor Learning and Control.* Dubuque: Brown.

Schultz. 1932. *Autogenics Training (Concentrative Self-Relaxation): Attempt at a Practical Clinical Presentation.* Leipzig: Thieme.

Selk, J. 2009. *10-Minute Toughness: The Mental-Training Program for Winning Before the Game Begins.* New York: McGraw-Hill.

Shiell, R. 2011. "Duke coach Mike Krzyzewski on his motivational techniques." July 18. Retrieved from http://bleacherreport.com/articles/770833-duke-coach-mike-krzyzewski-on-his-motivational-techniques.

Sinek, Simon. "How great leaders inspire action." Ted video, 18:04. Filmed September 2009. https://www.ted.com/talks/simon_sinek_how_great_leaders_inspire_action.

Skinner, B. F. 1969. *Contingencies of Reinforcement: A Theoretical Analysis.* New York: Meredith.

Smith, R. E., F. L. Smoll, and B. Curtis. 1979. "Coach effectiveness training: A cognitive-behavioral approach to relationship skills in youth sport coaches." *Journal of Sport Psychology* 1: 59–75.

Smith, R. E., F. L. Smoll, and M. W. Passer. 2002. "Sport Performance Anxiety in Children and Youth." In *Children and Youth in Sports: A Biopsychosocial Perspective,* 2nd ed., edited by F. L. Smoll and R. E. Smith, 501–536. Dubuque: Kendall/Hunt.

Spielberger, C. D. 1975. "The Measurement of State and Trait Anxiety: Conceptual and Methodological Issues." In *Emotions: Their Parameters and Measurement*, edited by L. Levi. New York: Raven Press.

Stahl, B. and E. Goldstein. 2010. *A Mindfulness-Based Stress Reduction Workbook.* Oakland: New Harbinger Publications.

Suinn, R. M. 1972. "Behavior rehearsal training for ski racers." *Behavior Therapy* 13: 519.

Suinn, R. M. 1984. "Visual motor behavior rehearsal: The basic technique." *Scandinavian Journal of Behaviour Therapy* 13: 131–142.

Summitt, Pat, and Sally Jenkins. *Reach for the Summit*. New York: Broadway Books.

Thorndike, E. L. *The Elements of Psychology*. New York: A. G. Seilor.

Tod, D., J. Hardy, and E. Oliver. 2011. "Effects of self-talk: A systematic review." *Journal of Exercise and Sport Psychology* 33 (2011): 666–687.

Weinberg, R., D. Burton, D. Yukelson, and D. Weigand. 2000. "Perceived goal setting practices of Olympic athletes: An exploratory investigation." *The Sport Psychologist* 14: 279–295.

Weinberg, R., and J. Butt. 2010 "Making goals effective: A primer for coaches." *Journal of Sport Psychology in Action* 1 (2): 57–65.

Weinberg, R. S. and D. Gould. 2011. *Foundations of Sport and Exercise Psychology*, 5th ed. Champaign: Human Kinetics.

Welz, K. 1991. http://www.welz.us/Autogenic.pdf.

Widmeyer, W. N., L. R. Brawley, and A. V. Carron. 1990. "The effects of group size in sport." *Journal of Exercise and Sport Psychology* 12: 177–190.

Widmeyer, W. N., A. V. Carron, and L. R. Brawley. 1993. "Group Cohesion in Sport and Exercise." In *Handbook of Research on Sport Psychology,* edited by R. Singer, M. Murphey, and L. Tennant. New York: Macmillan.

Williams, J. M. and V. Krane. 2015. *Applied Sport Psychology,* 7th ed. New York: McGraw-Hill.

Wolpe, J. 1969. *The Practice of Behavior Therapy.* New York: Pergamon Press.

Yukelson, D., and R. Rose. 2014. "The psychology of ongoing excellence: An NCAA coach's perspective on winning consecutive multiple national championships." *Journal of Sport Psychology in Action* 5.

Zourbanos, N., A. Hatzigeorgiadis, N. Tsiakaras, S. Chroni, and Y. Theodorakis. 2010. "A multi-method examination of the relationship between coaching behavior and athletes' inherent self-talk." *Journal of Sport and Exercise Psychology* 32: 764–785.

Team-Building Games Internet Sources

http://wheniwork.com/blog/team-building-games.

http://www.ultimatecampresource.com/site/camp-activities/team-building-games-and-initiatives.page-1.html.

http://www.teambuildingportal.com/games.

https://www.huddle.com/blog/team-building-activities.

About the Author

Mary Fenerty Schumann is a clinical and sport psychologist from Vienna, Virginia. She teaches sport psychology and works with athletes and teams at George Mason University. At George Mason, she has taught mental training skills and team building to several Division I teams, including basketball (men's and women's), softball, women's volleyball, wrestling, and women's soccer. Additionally, she trains athletes and teams to use mindfulness skills to help them effectively deal with their emotional reactions during performance. Dr. Schumann has taught at the college level for twenty years. Part of her professional work involves teaching visiting international athletes and coaches as a part of the Sports United/Sports Diplomacy program sponsored by the US Department of State.

In addition to her academic activities, Dr. Schumann maintains a busy clinical practice, seeing adolescents and adults. She draws from mindfulness-based stress reduction, cognitive behavioral therapy, and acceptance and commitment therapy approaches, teaching stress management skills in the process. Often she works with young athletes as well as former athletes. Dr. Schumann studied psychology at the University of Connecticut and obtained her master's and PhD in clinical psychology from Virginia Commonwealth University. Her dissertation involved studying adolescent problem behavior on a prevention grant called Athletes Coaching Teens. This program trained high school athletes to lead a goal-setting program for middle school kids in Richmond, Virginia.

Index

A

academic performance
coaching tips for, 151
overview, 143–151
academic success, 144, 145
acceptance and commitment
therapy (ACT), 102, 146
achievement-oriented goals, 49
affirming thoughts, 148
amotivation, 39
ANS (autonomic nervous
system), 87
anxiety
arousal and, 85–105
autogenics training to help
manage, 98–99
changes in attention,
concentration,
and visual search

arousal
and anxiety, 85–105
coaching tips for, 106
defined, 86–87

when experiencing
anxiety, 89–90
coaching tips for, 106
dealing with anxiety in
athletes, 90–92
deep diaphragmatic
breathing to help
manage, 97–98, 110
defined, 87–88
mindfulness meditation
to help manage,
100–105
progressive muscle
relaxation (PMR)
to help manage,
92–96
relaxation training to help
manage, 92–93
signs of, 88
state anxiety, 88, 89
trait anxiety, 88–89, 110

athletes, of today
compared to of
earlier times, xi–xii

athletic scholarships, danger of, 40

athletic success, academic success compared to, 144

audio recordings, for progressive muscle relaxation (PMR), 93

authoritarian/authoritative parenting, 5–7, 8

autogenics training, 98–99

autonomic nervous system (ANS), 87

B

Bandura, Albert, 60, 61

Barnett, F. T., 25, 26

Battier, Shane, 37–38

Baumrind, Diana, 5, 8

Beilock, Sian, 108, 111, 113

belief, importance of, 92

Bikram (hot) yoga, 77

Bilas, Jay, 120

body language, 13

body scan, 98, 101

box breathing, 97

Brawley, L. R., 73

Brennan, Stephen, 38

Brown, Dale, 130

C

Cameron, Kim, 16–17

career fairs, 148

Carron, A. V., 72, 73

cell phones, behavioral impact of, 135–136

centering breath, 97, 114

"Centering Breath Exercise," 103–104, 145

Choke: What the Secrets of the Brain Reveal About Getting It Right When You Have To (Beilock), 108

choking
coaching tips for, 114–115
overview, 107–115

Clifton Strengths Finder, 148

coaching, styles of, 2, 4–9

cognitive behavioral therapy, 102

cohesion
coaching tips for, 79–81
defined, 72
factors of, 75–77
games to build cohesion, 82–84

cohesion dynamics, 72–73

collective efficacy, 60, 64

communication
coaching tips for, 17–18
of John Wooden, 31–32
negative communication, 16, 36
nonverbal communication, 9, 12–13
overview, 1–17
positive communication, 16, 36

verbal communication, ix, xi, 11–12, 13
Competitive Excellence (Brennan), 38
confidence
    coaching tips for, 67–69
    self-efficacy and, 59–69
continuous reinforcement, 21
credibility, 14
Cuddy, Amy, 13

D

Davis, Hap, 113
deep diaphragmatic breathing, 97–98, 110
democratic parenting, 6
desensitization, 108–109
digital natives, 134–138
Drive (Pink), 147
Dweck, Carol, 128, 146–147

E

Eklund, R. C., 65
Emmons, R. A., 122
entity theory, 147
external rewards, 39, 41
extrinsic motivation, 36, 39–41

F

Facebook, 136, 137
failure quotient (F.Q.), 130–131
fear of failure, 25, 39
feedback, 29–32, 34
"5-Minute Mindful Breathing Meditation," 100
fixed mind-set, 128

fixed-interval schedule, 22
fixed-ratio schedule, 21–22
four-square breathing, 97
Frederickson, Barbara, 16

G

Gallimore, R., 31
games, to build cohesion, 82–84
Gardner, Frank, 52, 102, 105, 146
goal setting
    overview, 47–50
    realistic goal setting, 50–52
goals
    defined, 48
    importance of self-determination of, 52
    measurement of, 54–56
    in positive terms, 54
    practice and competition goals, 53–54
    role of, 48
    short-term and long-term goals, 52–53
    SMART goals, 49
    Smart Goals (app), 53–54
    task goals, 49, 50
    tips on setting of, 56–57

Goals on Track (app), 53–54
Goldstein, Elisha, 100
Gould, D., 65
grateful attitude, 122–123
gratitude journal, 122
Greenspan, Stephen, 8
growth mind-set
    coaching tips for, 131–132
    development of, 130–131
    winning with, 128–130

H

Hanin, Y. L., 69, 87
Hanton, S., 67
Hatfield, Bradley D., 112–113
helpless response, 148
helplessness, 26
high-pressure training
    situations, 91
hopelessness, 26
human knot (game), 83

I

individualized zone of optimal
    functioning (ZOF or
    IZOF), 69, 87
Instagram, 136, 137
internal rewards, 40
intrinsic motivation, 36, 39–41

J

Jackson, Phil, xii, 101
Jackson, R. C., 65
Jackson, Robin, 111
Johnson, Mark, 38–39

Jones, G., 67
Jordan, Michael, 121

K

Kabat-Zinn, Jon, xii, 100, 105
Kaufmann, Keith, 105
Knight, Bobby, 5
Komaki, J., 25, 26
Krzyzewski, Mike (Coach K),
    7, 37–38

L

Latham, G. P., 55
learning, fostering of, 144–151
Lewis, Catherine, 8
Lift (app), 53–54
Locke, Edwin, 48, 55
Longshore, Kat, xiii

M

MAC approach, 105
Martens, Rainer, 14, 140, 141
mastery oriented, 148
MBSR (mindfulness-based
    stress reduction), xii,
    100, 102, 105
McCullough, M. E., 122
meditation, xii, 44. See also
    mindfulness meditation
mental toughness, 27, 77, 129
The Mindful Athlete
    (Mumford), xii, 101
mindfulathleticperformance.
    com (author's
    website), 157

mindfulness
    benefits of, 63, 90
    defined, xii
    use of, xii–xiii, 68, 145
Mindfulness for Sport
    Performance
    Enhancement, 105
mindfulness meditation, xii,
    xiii, 100–105, 110
"Mindfulness of the Breath
    Exercise," 102–103, 145
*Mindfulness-Based Stress
    Reduction: A Workbook*
    (Goldstein and
    Stahl), 100
mindfulness-based stress
    reduction (MBSR), xii,
    100, 102, 105
mind-set
    and academic achievement,
        146–147
    fixed mind-set, 128
    growth mind-set, 128–132
    overview, 127–128
    survey questionnaire
        on, 129
*Mindset: The New Psychology of
    Success* (Dweck), 128
Moore, Zella, 52, 102, 105, 146
motivation
    amotivation, 39
    coaching tips for, 44–45
    extrinsic motivation, 36,
        39–41
    intrinsic motivation, 36,
        39–41

    overview, 35–45
    self-directed
        motivation, 40
    wellness and, 43–44
motivational transitions, 42–43
Mumford, George, xii, 63, 101
Mussina, Mike, 110

N

negative communication,
    16, 36
negative reinforcement, 24, 36
negative self-talk, 66
negativity, cautions with, 16
next play, 120
nonverbal communication, 9,
    12–13

O

"the One-Minute Drill," 32
open-door policy, 4
optimal functioning,
    individualized zone of
    (ZOF or IZOF), 69, 87
Optimize Me (app), 53–54
outcome goals, 49

P

paralysis by analysis, 111
parental guidelines, 141–142
parenting, styles of, 2, 4–9
parent-orientation meeting,
    140–141

parents
    and technology, coaching
        tips for, 142
    and technology, overview,
        133–142
partial reinforcement, 21
passiveness, 26–27
permissive parenting, 2, 5, 7–8
personal performance reel,
    124, 125
Pink, Daniel, 147
positive coaching, 19–34
positive communication, 16, 36
positive emotions, undoing
    effect of, 123
positive psychology, 16
positive reinforcement, 20–24,
    25–26, 27, 36, 37
positivity, importance of, 16
praise, 16, 22, 23, 25, 36, 130
progressive muscle relaxation
    (PMR), 92–96
*The Psychology of Enhancing
    Human Performance:
    The Mindfulness-
    Acceptance-Commitment
    Approach* (Gardner and
    Moore), 146
punishment, 5, 24–25, 28,
    40, 109

R

reframing, 91
Reid, Roger, 109
reinforcement
    coaching tips for, 33

continuous
    reinforcement, 21
negative reinforcement,
    24, 36
partial reinforcement, 21
positive reinforcement,
    20–24, 25–26, 27,
    36, 37
timing of, 32
use of, 20, 50
verbal and nonverbal
    communication as
    forms of, 13
reinforcers, 21, 23, 55
relaxation, 90, 98, 100. *See
    also* progressive muscle
    relaxation (PMR)
relaxation training, 92–93
Remember the Titans (film),
    5, 80
respect
    developing lack of respect,
        8, 15
    generating of, 4, 28
    importance of, 7, 8, 15,
        74–75
rewards, 20, 22, 23, 25–26,
    27, 28, 39, 40–41, 50,
    78, 145
Robinson, Frank, 121
Rose, Russ, 32
rules
    coaching tips for, 33–34
    setting and enforcing of,
        28–29

S

sandwich approach, 32
Schulz, Dr., 98
self-determination, 41
self-determination theory (SDT), 39
self-directed motivation, 40
self-efficacy
    as affecting our view of challenges, 64
    coaching tips for, 67–69
    and confidence, 59–69
    factors in, 60–63
self-regulation, 144–145, 148
self-talk, 64–67, 88, 112
Seligman, Martin, 16
Selk, Jason, 97, 110, 114, 124
shared adversity, 76
Sinek, Simon, 50
Skinner, B. F., 20–21, 23
slumps
    coaching tips for, 125
    counteracting of, 122–124
    defined, 118
    origins of, 118–122
SMART goals, 49
Smart Goals (app), 53–54
Snapchat, 136
social cohesion, 73, 74–75
social persuasion, 62
sports diplomacy program (US Department of State), x
square-box breathing, 97
Stahl, Jonathan, 100
state anxiety, 88, 89

Successful Coaching (Martens), 14, 140, 141
Suinn, R. M., 124
Summitt, Pat, 3, 75

T

tact and diplomacy, regarding parents and technology issues, 138–142
task cohesion, 73–74
task goals, 49, 50
task performance, goal setting as helping with, 48
team cohesion, 71–84
team norms, 77–79
technology
    parents and, coaching tips for, 142
    parents and, overview, 133–142
10-Minute Toughness (Selk), 97, 110, 124
texting, 135–136
Tharp, R., 31
Toughness: Developing True Strength On and Off the Court (Bilas), 120
trait anxiety, 88–89, 110
Twitter, 137

U

undoing effect of positive emotions, 123
US Department of State sports diplomacy program, x

V

variable-interval schedule, 22
variable-ratio schedule, 22
verbal communication, ix, xi,
    11–12, 13
verbal persuasion, 60, 92
visual motor behavioral
    rehearsal (VMBR), 124
visualization, 123–124

W

Weinberg, R. S., 52
wellness, and motivation,
    43–44
Widmeyer, W. N., 73
withholding information,
    cautions with, 10
Wooden, John, 7, 31–32
work ethic, 27

Y

yoga, 77, 98, 105
yogic breathing, 97
Yukelson, David, 32

Z

ZOF or IZOF (individualized
    zone of optimal
    functioning), 69, 87

Printed in the United States
By Bookmasters